MORE PRAISE FOR Making A Difference: 365 Tips, Ideas and Stories to Change Your World

"Picture starting every day for one whole year by asking yourself one simple question, 'What can I do today to make a difference in the lives of others?" Now, imagine if everyone in your community daily asked themselves the same thing? The results would be extraordinary. Lisa Dietlin's newest work is a valuable resource for our nation's philanthropic sector. These daily bite-sized nuggets will expose, educate, inspire and motivate every reader to action. One of my favorites appears on page 214 and reminds us that charity is rooted in an important childhood value: "Philanthropy," Dietlin notes, "is a grown up word for sharing." This book relays inspirational quotations, historical perspectives, startling statistics and innovative ideas all laser-focused on helping you, the reader, find innovative ways to create transformation in your life and community through the simple act of doing good."

Robert B. Acton EXECUTIVE DIRECTOR, CABRINI GREEN LEGAL AID
Adjunct Professor in Non Profit Leadership and Management, DePaul University School

"You will like many of the specific ideas, suggestions, and inspirational quotes in this book and find them helpful. But even more importantly, the sheer volume and variety of them gives us hope. There are so many ways to "make a difference"—to help others and in doing so help oneself become a better, more fulfilled person. Lisa Dietlin's book shows that throughout this country and the world thousands of people and organizations are working to create a better future. Now you have no excuse not to participate."

Wim Wiewel PRESIDENT
Portland State University

"*Making A Difference* Tips of the Day aligns incredibly with medical science, demonstrating that charitable giving can be directed toward proven methods of preventing human maladies. Kudos to author Dietlin for tapping into smart giving!"

Allan P. Frank, MD, MS, INTERNAL MEDICINE,
Former Director of Clinical Research at both Abbott Laboratories and Roche Molecular Systems.

Books and More that Make the World Better

www.networlding.com

John —

Keep making a difference!

Best!

[signature]

Dedication

This book is dedicated to four people who have made a difference in my life ~

To my siblings Linda and Jeffrey — you taught me how to share my toys, my secrets, my joys, my laughs and my tears! Thanks for always, always being there for me! Being part of your lives has made all the difference in my life!

To my sister-in-law, Danielle — you joined the family and that made all the difference in the world!

To my Uncle Don...with much love! Please know that you did make a difference!

Acknowledgments

I still believe it takes a village to write a book! Many people helped to make this book a reality and for that I am deeply grateful. First, thanks must be given to my staff. When I said that I was writing another book they lent their support wholeheartedly, never asking.... what are you doing and where will you find the time to do it? Thank you Julie, Stephanie, Barbara, Katherine, Lisa, Kris, Kristie and others for your support! Thank you also to Nadine for editing my book not once or twice but three times!! You made a difference and the process of writing a bit easier!

Thank you also to my friends who lent their support again never questioning the cancelled lunches, short phone conversations and text messages instead of emails...they knew I was on a mission and for that I am grateful!

Thanks must also be given to my Facebook friends. What started out as an idea has turned into a book. To everyone who posted a comment, like or made a suggestion to my Charity Tips of the Day, you gave me the idea that this type of book was needed in the world!

Thank you also to my good girlfriends Valerie Ingram, Mary Ann Beckwith, Karen Hynes, Margaret Soffin, Evelyn Ward, Renee Torina, Cathy Shook, Annette Lozon, Caroline Coppola, Aimee Daniels, Suzanne Jurva, Julia Koch, Erin Minne', Nadine Donajkowski, Annette Cox, Angie Noble, Cathy Brod, Marlie Sailer, Jan Pruitt, Abby McWilliams, Emmie Ruffin, Sherry Hooper, Hallie Crawford, Cibeline Sariano, Leticia Herrera, Barbara Figgins, Kathryn Tack, Sandra Mattison and Janet Katowitz...**thank you** for being on this journey with me! Your friendship and support have made a difference in my life!

Finally, thank you to everyone who works or at least tries to make a difference in their family, community or world. While at times, your efforts might seem to go unnoticed, **you do make a difference!**

Introduction

I had barely finished writing my first book when I began thinking about the second one I would write. It didn't seem a matter of "if" I would write a second book, but rather "when". What I have learned during the last year is that I am a good story teller and that's what this book is....a compilation of stories about experiences, nonprofits, individuals, groups and organizations. The one thing they all have in common is that they are trying to make a difference in this world. In one way or another each tip, idea or story gives a glimpse into what really matters in life.

As the saying goes, "Life's not the breaths you take, but the moments that take your breath away!"

What takes your breath away?

I hope throughout the next year you will take time each day to read the daily tip. I hope that tip will encourage you to work to make a difference. I hope that you will write your thoughts on the experience or attempts to make a difference. And finally, I hope that like the last tip in this book, your efforts will result in ripples in a pond after the stone has been thrown....

Make A Difference!

Lisa M. Dietlin
NOVEMBER 2010

Most individuals give away about 2% of their household income. However, Tom and Bree Hsieh, Robert Schoenhall and his wife Jill Warren and Richard Semmler do much more giving away 25 to 60% of their income annually? Why do they do this? According to *The Chronicle of Philanthropy* article, they are committed to giving back and making a difference. Is there something you can do to increase your commitment to charity and make a bigger difference?

TIP OF THE DAY

During the recession, 21 states added jobs in the nonprofit sector while in those same states companies cut jobs according to a recent study. Another report showed the average total annual compensation for a nonprofit CEO/Executive Director is $115,138! Check the nonprofit sector for job opportunities when considering a new job. Your daily work would make a difference!

Making a Difference

Cabrini Green Legal Aid (www.cgla.net) is a non-profit clinic with the mission of assuring justice and mercy to the poorest in Chicago. The organization provides legal services in four areas: family, housing, criminal records and criminal defense. Founded in 1973 to serve primarily the residents of the Cabrini Green projects, it now serves the Greater Chicago area with clients finding their way to the Clinic from distant suburbs. Hundreds of lawyers, individuals and others volunteer their time annually to insure legal services are available. CGLA is definitely making a difference!

Making a Difference

Tooth decay is the most common chronic childhood disease in the US. Actor Chris O'Donnell joined forces with Trident gum to raise funds for Smiles Across America, a program of the nonprofit Oral Health America providing dental services to children. We often do not think of our health in terms of teeth but perhaps we should! How can you make a difference resulting in healthy teeth?

_____

_____

_____

_____

_____

_____

_____

_____

_____

_____

_____

Making a Difference

Daily we hear how the economy is doing including the car companies. Ford Motor is doing more than making cars these days; it is committed to the fight against breast cancer by giving more than $105 million over 16 years. Ford created the Warriors in Pink wear/gear with the proceeds going to the Susan G. Komen for the Cure. Check it out at www.fordcares.com and join the effort to make a difference!

Making a Difference

Many of us have heard that Facebook founder Mark Zuckerberg has made a $100 million donation to the Newark Public Schools. This is an unbelievable gift!! What makes me sad is the media questioning why Mark made the gift. I think they are missing the point. A 26 year old made a $100 million gift — let us talk about the example Mark is setting and how his gift will make a difference!

Making a Difference

My mother gave me a card with the following quote on it from Henry Van Dyke (born in 1852) who was an American author, educator and clergyman, "There is a loftier ambition than merely to stand high in the world. It is to stoop down and lift mankind a little higher." I love this statement and what it communicates! Today, try to make a difference to someone in your world!

_____

_____

_____

_____

_____

_____

_____

_____

_____

_____

_____

_____

Making a Difference

I recently heard a radio production of the play *12 Angry Men*. While listening I was reminded how 1 person makes a difference. The play is about a jury debating the fate of a young man. Initially, eleven (11) jurors believe he is guilty. But one juror votes not guilty and because of this one man, a difference is made in a young man's life. Think about your actions today and how you can make a difference!

_____

_____

_____

_____

_____

_____

_____

_____

_____

_____

_____

Making a Difference

Have you heard about 79 year old Mary Haith Savage? She lives in Pittsburgh and is known as the Flower Lady because for 40 years she has been focused on turning vacant lots of land into beautiful gardens. She reportedly does not like the term flower lady because to her it is about the community and doing what she has to do to make the area more livable! Thanks, Mary, for making a difference!

_____

_____

_____

_____

_____

_____

_____

_____

_____

_____

_____

Making a Difference

According to a 2010 report, about one third of all US students do not graduate from high school and for Latino or African American boys the rate jumps to 50%! We must do better! Denzel Washington is the national spokesperson for Boys and Girls Clubs crediting BGC for helping him dream big dreams! When was the last time you stopped by your local BGC? Check it out and see if you can make a difference!

_____

_____

_____

_____

_____

_____

_____

_____

_____

_____

Making a Difference

According to a recent study by the Russ Reid Company, children really do what they see their parents doing, at least in charitable efforts. The study revealed that the charitable habits of parents really do affect the likelihood of kids becoming a donor to nonprofits by more than 80%! Thanks to all parents who are charitable and making a huge difference in the lives of their children!

Making a Difference

When in Santa Fe, I attended the Annual Burning of Zozobra (www.zozobra.com) (Zozobra is reportedly a Native American word for gloom). This event sponsored by the Kiwanis raises money for scholarships. More than 25,000 people came out to watch old man gloom burn taking with him all the bad things from the previous year. Check it out and see how a unique event raises money and makes a difference!

Making a Difference

In 1986, the actor Ted Danson he took his daughters to the beach. They arrived to find the Will Rogers State Beach closed because of pollution. This outraged Ted and he decided to do something about it. He co-founded the American Oceans Campaign which has since merged with Oceana and is doing something about things such as mercury contamination and offshore wind energy. Thanks for making a difference, Ted!

Making a Difference

September 11th is a date that causes us to remember where we were, what we were doing and most important, how we felt. If you are like most people, you came to a sudden realization that it didn't matter how many material things you had, what mattered was did you make a difference? Remember that feeling today while continuing to make a difference for others!

_____

_____

_____

_____

_____

_____

_____

_____

_____

_____

Making a Difference

The actor Christopher Reeve said, "I think a hero is an ordinary individual who finds strength to persevere and endure in spite of overwhelming obstacles." After his horse riding accident, Christopher Reeve and his wife, Dana, worked to make a difference to those with spinal cord injuries. What needs to be done in your community? What is affecting you? How could you be a hero and make a difference?!

_____

_____

_____

_____

_____

_____

_____

_____

_____

_____

Making a Difference

Have you seen the commercials about Stand Up To Cancer? It is an effort by more than 70 artists and all the major TV networks to raise funds for collaborative cancer research. By working together, money was raised and they did make a difference!

Making a Difference

TIP OF THE DAY

Back on My Feet is a support group for homeless people, many of whom are drug and alcohol addicted. The mission is to help get their lives in order by instilling discipline through running while improving their health and self esteem. Started in Philadelphia by Anne Mahlum after she daily ran by a homeless shelter and began talking with the men, it is now going national and truly making a difference!

Making a Difference

One in three (1 in 3) women have heart disease and more than 64% do not have any symptoms before their first heart attack! Women: Learn the warning signs and get involved in preventing death by heart disease, the leading cause of death for women! The American Heart Association is working to change this and to make a difference!

_____

_____

_____

_____

_____

_____

_____

_____

_____

_____

_____

Making a Difference

The actress Sandra Bullock is helping rebuild her beloved New Orleans. She's involved with the Warren Easton Charter High School both as a donor and as an advocate! Destroyed after Hurricane Katrina, the school has rebuilt and recently opened a health clinic funded by the Kellogg Foundation, the San Francisco 49ers and Sandra Bullock. Thanks Sandra for leading by example and making a difference!

Making a Difference

As a kid I remember watching the Jerry Lewis Telethon for Muscular Dystrophy during the Labor Day holiday weekend. While the telethon's visibility has diminished, it's still raising money with more than $65 million raised last year. In 60 years of hosting it, Jerry has helped raise nearly $6.5 billion. Jerry Lewis is still making a difference. This is still a way to make a difference!

_____

_____

_____

_____

_____

_____

_____

_____

_____

_____

Making a Difference

Storycorps is a nonprofit whose mission is to provide all Americans with the opportunity to tell, record and share their story. It's the largest oral history project with the recordings being saved at the Library of Congress. Since 2003, more than 60,000 people have participated — mothers and sons, husbands and wives, etc.— coming together to share a story. Share your story and make a difference!

Making a Difference

Have you heard of the Ploughshares Fund? It is the largest US grant making foundation wholly dedicated to security and peace funding. For over 25 years they have funded research, scientists and efforts to prevent the spread and use of nuclear weapons. They focus on building regional peace and stability. Check it out to see how a group of dedicated individuals are working to make a difference!

_____

_____

_____

_____

_____

_____

_____

_____

_____

The Michigan County Social Services Association is a nonprofit organization leading and providing support to Michigan's neediest citizens. It's amazing to see 150 people sharing ideas and learning how to be more effective in delivering services such as foster care/adult care, insuring access to food, etc. These individuals, from my home state, are truly making a difference!

Making a Difference

After Hurricane Katrina hit, the actor Brad Pitt got involved and stay focused on what was needed to rebuild New Orleans, especially the Lower 9th Ward. Frustrated by the slow pace, in 2007 he started the Make It Right Foundation. To date, nearly 50 homes that are green and can withstand a category 4 storm have been built and more than 200 people have come home! Thanks Brad for making a difference!

Making a Difference

Recently, I learned about the Treetops hotel and staff efforts to change the lives of kids in foster care. The hotel and its staff raise money donating it to the local social services agency. The agency uses the funds to purchase and provide things to kids in the foster care system—things like bicycles, baseball and/or soccer equipment — items they don't usually have. Now, that's making a difference!

Making a Difference

I read a quote by Robert F. Kennedy that I thought was a perfect way to start each day: "Each time someone stands up for an ideal, or acts to improve the lot of others, or strikes out against injustice, he sends forth a tiny ripple of hope." I know if you do one of these things today, you will make a difference!

_____

_____

_____

_____

_____

_____

_____

_____

_____

_____

_____

_____

Making a Difference

Even though our combat soldiers withdrew from Iraq in 2010, there are still soldiers working there during this transition time. Let's not forget our soldiers. Recently, I learned from my mom that she and some friends are still putting together care packages for our soldiers in Iraq and Afghanistan. Spend some time thinking about how to support our soldiers and make a difference!

Making a Difference

The famous author Ralph Waldo Emerson said, "What lies behind us and what lies before us are tiny matters compared to what lies within us." What lies within you to make a difference?

_____

_____

_____

_____

_____

_____

_____

_____

_____

_____

_____

_____

_____

Making a Difference

Started in 1926, February is Black History Month. The purpose is the remembrance of important people and events in African American history. Take time to learn more about a history many of us never studied in school — attend functions, watch news programs and read to learn more. By becoming aware of others' histories, we learn more about ourselves and can make a difference!

_____

_____

_____

_____

_____

_____

_____

_____

_____

_____

_____

TIP OF THE DAY

To do my part to clean the environment, everyday I pick up at least one piece of trash or garbage that I see on the ground and place it in the appropriate trash receptacle. It's amazing how good I feel about doing this simple thing to clean up my world. I can do it during my morning exercise walk or when I'm running through an airport to catch a plane. It's an easy way to make a difference.

Making a Difference

While most parents will be getting kids ready to go back to school buying backpacks, notebooks, pencils, calculators, crayons, etc., there will be families that aren't able to do this given the economy. Consider purchasing two of everything and donating the second set of items to your child's classroom or school in order to help someone else's child. That would be making a difference!!!

The grocery store chain, Whole Foods, is campaigning to put 300 salad bars in schools. With donations from the company and customers, the funds will allow Chef Ann Cooper to put a salad bar in a school near each of the Whole Foods stores in the US. They're encouraging discussions about salad bars and the importance of nutrition while working to make a difference one school at a time!

Making a Difference

Pakistan experienced its worst flooding in years. It was estimated that more than 20% of Pakistan is flooded. This has affected 14 million people...6 million of them children. Food, clean water and health supplies are needed immediately. You can help by making a charitable donation to UNICEF USA (www.unicefusa.org). You will be making a difference!

Making a Difference

Many think *and* the challenges facing us are unprecedented ~~but we~~ wonder what we can do to help. Where do we begin? Have you heard about www.Serve.gov? Check it out to find a volunteer opportunity, register your project, read an inspiring story or share your inspiring story. You may find a way to make a difference!

Making a Difference

In 2009, my first book was published! It's titled *Transformational Philanthropy: Entrepreneurs and Nonprofits* and details how nonprofits and entrepreneurs can work together better. Did you know 85 – 88% of all the money donated annually comes from individuals, including entrepreneurs? Read my book to learn more about working with nonprofits and how 23 entrepreneurs are making a difference!

_____

_____

_____

_____

_____

_____

_____

_____

_____

_____

Making a Difference

Have you heard of Meatless Mondays? This is a redo of a World War I campaign to ration food staples. Meatless Mondays and Wheatless Wednesdays were marketed as ways to "...win the war." Today Meatless Mondays is an effort to improve our health and help our planet by reducing overall consumption. Check out the nonprofit (www.meatlessmondays.com) to see if you can join the effort and make a difference!

Making a Difference

TIP OF THE DAY

People think the charitable world is a small niche not affecting many. I challenge each of you to count the number of times in a 48 hour period you see, hear, read or run into something that has a charitable component. You will be amazed! Take this time to notice how often others are trying to make a difference!

A simple way to make a difference is at the post office. When you are purchasing a book of stamps buy and extra book and donate them to your favorite nonprofit.

Making a Difference

By now most of us have heard of the Pepsi Refresh Project. This was Pepsi's yearlong effort to encourage us to get involved as well as provide funding for local projects. What an innovative and great way for a corporation to get involved and make a difference while involving others!

Making a Difference

Have you heard of the DAV — Disabled American Veterans group? This nonprofit exists to serve the country's disabled veterans, their dependents and survivors. With 88 offices throughout the country, the DAV works to assist veterans in filing VA claims free of charge, information sessions, counseling and community outreach. Check it out at www.dav.org and see how the DAV is making a difference!

Making a Difference

In order to help the environment and hopefully do my part to reduce global warming, I try one day a week not to use or even move my car. On that day, I walk, take public transportation or simply stay home and enjoy my house and neighborhood. I often wonder what would happen if we all did this. I think it would definitely make a difference in your life and to the environment! Will you try it?

_____

_____

_____

_____

_____

_____

_____

_____

_____

_____

_____

_____

Making a Difference

The other day I needed an extension ladder to hang a piece of art; I didn't have one and wasn't sure any of my neighbors would have one I could borrow. Then I heard about neighborgoods.net, started by Micki Krimmel to facilitate people sharing things with each other — the way neighbors used to do. Check it out...you might make a difference by sharing what you have with someone else!

Making a Difference

Share Your Soles began when Mona Purdy saw kids in Central America put tar on the bottom of their feet to protect them. They did this because they didn't have shoes. What started as a single good deed turned into an effort that has distributed more than one (1) million shoes in eleven (11) years. Check out www.shareyoursoles.org and consider donating a pair or two of your shoes to help someone and make a difference!

Have you heard about generosity based publishing via Concord Publishing? I just learned that authors, who may be having trouble getting their books published, choose to give it away asking the person who receives the book to make a donation to their favorite cause. Check it out at www.concordfreepress.com. What a way to make a difference!

_____

_____

_____

_____

_____

_____

_____

_____

_____

_____

_____

Making a Difference

Are you wondering what you can do to make a difference this week? How about donating blood? There is always a high demand for O-Negative blood but as usual all blood types are needed. Go to the American Red Cross website (www.redcross.org) to find your local chapter. Call today to schedule an appointment. You can make a difference!

_____

_____

_____

_____

_____

_____

_____

_____

_____

_____

Making a Difference

Recently, I learned from my friend Barbara about Anne Marie Schlekeway, an extraordinary person who is outgoing, funny and loud! Five years ago she was diagnosed with ALS — Lou Gehrig's Disease. She decided to live her life by communicating through a medium other than her voice creating a new business as well as a blog called Kiss My ALS! Check it out and watch a recent interview at www.kissmyals.com. She is making a difference!

Making a Difference

Have you seen the "Be the One" commercial? Women of the Storm, a grassroots organization formed after Hurricanes Katrina/Rita came up with the idea of encouraging people to sign a petition demanding funding to protect the Gulf, coastal region and wetlands. Check out the video and consider signing the petition at www.restorethegulf. com. You can "be the one" that makes a difference!

Making a Difference

I saw an amazing commercial about animals being rescued from abusive situations. Check out the Humane Society website (www.humanesociety.org) to see how you can assist in rescuing animals from disasters, preventing dog fighting and eliminating puppy mills. For many, animals are an important part of their lives. By learning more, you can make a difference by making a donation or adopting an animal.

Making a Difference

Life is about choices. What choices will you make today and how will they affect others? Consider being purposeful today about your charitable acts. Who can you help, what can you change...in other words, how can you make a difference?

_____

_____

_____

_____

_____

_____

_____

_____

_____

_____

_____

_____

TIP OF THE DAY

Former President Woodrow Wilson said, "Provision for others is a fundamental responsibility of human life." I totally agree. Start your week off by thinking of how you can help one other person each day. By doing this you will truly be making a difference!

TIP OF THE DAY

We are bombarded daily with news of job losses. Have you thought about searching for a job or career in the nonprofit sector? One reason to consider this is that research has shown people working in the nonprofit sector are happier than those who work in the government and for-profit sectors. It makes sense because if you work in the nonprofit sector you are part of making a difference everyday!

_____

_____

_____

_____

_____

_____

_____

_____

_____

_____

_____

_____

Making a Difference

I recently read about Albert Pujols, the St. Louis Cardinals' first baseman — not only is he often voted MVP, but he does amazing work in the Dominican Republic to give back. He takes dentists, doctors and other professionals to the Dominican Republic to help the children. Learn more about his humanitarian work; he's definitely making a difference!

_____

_____

_____

_____

_____

_____

_____

_____

_____

_____

Making a Difference

In summer, many of us forget about the important work nonprofits are still doing. Foodbanks are still feeding people, environmental restoration is still taking place, theater companies are working on their fall productions and the list goes on. Today think about your favorite cause and find a way to make a difference!

_____

_____

_____

_____

_____

_____

_____

_____

_____

_____

_____

_____

Making a Difference

The YMCA announced a name change in 2010 — going forward it will simply be known as the "Y". Founded 166 years ago and named the Young Men's Christian Association, the Y is revamping its image and hoping folks will know about its focus on youth, healthy living and communities. When was the last time you visited a Y Center? Check it out in your community — find out how the Y is making a difference!

_____

_____

_____

_____

_____

_____

_____

_____

_____

_____

Making a Difference

Much of Haiti was devastated by an earthquake. While the news media is not covering the situation everyday, there are still daily if not hourly needs. Make it a point today to do something about it — donate money, volunteer or simply talk about it to your friends and colleagues to keep it in front of people. There are still needs and definitely ways to make a difference!

_____

_____

_____

_____

_____

_____

_____

_____

_____

_____

_____

March is Women's History Month. Did you know the YWCA was founded in 1876 by 13 women with a passion for empowering women and girls? The Girl Scouts was founded almost 100 years ago by one woman trying to make a difference in the lives of young girls. What can you do to honor our women heroes of the past? What can you do to help the young girls of the 21st century? Know that you can make a difference.

_____

_____

_____

_____

_____

_____

_____

_____

_____

_____

Making a Difference

Are you a wise consumer? Do you know the charitable participation of the companies from which you purchase products or services? It might seem insurmountable but why not decide to find out. Choose one company and make it your mission today to ask what they do to give back to the community. You'll be letting the company know giving back is important and you will be making a difference!

Making a Difference

Are you in college and looking for an alternative spring break? Approximately 72,000 students will participate in a spring break helping others. The nonprofit Break Away, which matches colleges with charities, says this is becoming a very popular way to spend time — doing things for others with jobs from laying sod to painting to serving food. Check it out; there are ways for all of us to make a difference!

Making a Difference

Mary Tyler Moore is still active serving as the International Chairman for the Juvenile Diabetes Research Foundation (www.jdrf.org). This is the nonprofit that conducts research on Type I diabetes which has had a staggering increase in the number of people who have this disease. JDRF's mission is to find a cure. Check it out and see how you can help to make a difference and eliminate this disease.

_____

_____

_____

_____

_____

_____

_____

_____

_____

TIP OF THE DAY

Most of us have heard of the USO probably in reference to the holiday Bob Hope USO tours. Did you know the USO is a nonprofit providing a "touch of home" to our soldiers? From free phone cards to care packages with much needed items, the USO is there to help and you can, too. Check out the USO website (www.uso.org) and consider making a donation. Your financial contribution will definitely make a difference!

Making a Difference

Donors give money to charity. Volunteers give time to charity. Board members must give both. Many board members don't realize their responsibilities of both money and time. In assessing your role with a charity are you in the right place? How are you making a difference?

_____

_____

_____

_____

_____

_____

_____

_____

_____

_____

_____

_____

TIP OF THE DAY

Do you have a meaningful summer project planned? Why not gather your friends and family together to volunteer on a project to help a charity? Decide over the next few days or weeks what you want to do, contact the nonprofit to make arrangements and get information needed to be successful. Then ask your friends/family to join you. What a wonderful way to spend time together and make a difference!

TIP OF THE DAY

Consider the wonder of living in the USA. Philanthropy became an established practice and eventually institution because our founders wanted schools, hospitals, libraries, etc. and realized they were going to have to make it happen. They stepped up and while founding a country also established a pattern of neighbor helping neighbor. Follow the practice of our founders and make a difference!

TIP OF THE DAY

Recently, I overheard a conversation about doing holiday shopping in July. It got me thinking of all the gifts we believe we need to buy for others on holidays, birthdays, etc. Why not make this the year you make a donation to your favorite charity in the person's name instead of buying a gift? Think about the difference you could make and you will save on buying gift bags and wrapping paper!

The nonprofit Do Something (www.Dosomething. org) has the tagline of "Powering offline action — using the power of online to get teens to do good stuff offline". Check it out; every week they give away a seed grant of $500 to jump start a program or realize an idea. Perhaps this is a way to begin teaching the next generation the power and importance of giving back. Teens can and do make a difference!

_____

_____

_____

_____

_____

_____

_____

_____

_____

_____

_____

Garage, yard and tag sales appear in summer — you can add a charitable component. Have a sale this year and donate the proceeds to your favorite charity. Alternately, donate the "unused" stuff you find in the house to the Goodwill, Salvation Army, etc. You'll be helping individuals/families as well as getting a tax deduction (remember to keep detailed records). Some easy ways to make a difference!

Heard about Crowdrise (www.crowdrise.com)? It was begun by actor and activist Edward Norton and two others. Crowdrise works to have social networking make giving go viral. Users build a profile and project pages while getting others to join them in raising money — similar to asking friends to sponsor you in a walk or marathon. It's a clever idea and it'll be interesting to watch. Check it out and see if you can make a difference!

TIP OF THE DAY

The Girl Scouts have been around for almost 100 years! I recently learned one of their mottos is, "What did you do today?" This question was asked of seven young girls on stage during a dinner with answers ranging from feeding people to collecting coats to mentoring and having the experience of being an engineer. What did you do today — to make a difference in your life and the lives of others?

With sadness I read about Ex — Bears Football player Chris Zorich and his nonprofit that is now in disarray. It's another example of someone wanting to good, in this case, help needy families, and not knowing how. In most communities there are experts working at your community foundation. Contact them and find out how best to make a difference in your community and achieve the results you want!

Food insecurity is a term coined by the US Department of Agriculture to describe situations whereby people do not know from where their next meal will come. Feeding America, the nation's network of food banks, works every day to insure that every person has access to food. Learn more about how to feed the hungry by going to www.feedingamerica.org. Through simply learning more about this issue you will be making a difference!

Making a Difference

In the aftermath of the Gulf Disaster, are you still wondering how can you help? Check out the nonprofit Matter of Trust (www.matteroftrust.org). They create "booms" of nylon stuffed with nature fibers such as hair and fur which are used to contain oil spills. They need assistance both in terms of financial donations and volunteers. Perhaps there is a way for you to make a difference by helping this group!

_____

_____

_____

_____

_____

_____

_____

_____

_____

Making a Difference

The actress Angela Lansbury has joined the fight to find a cure for ALS, more commonly known as Lou Gehrig's disease. She lost her sister to this devastating illness and now is committed to helping the ALS organization. My friend Keith had this terrible disease and died some years ago. Do you know someone who has this disease? Learn more about ALS (www.alsa.org) and find a way to make a difference!

When thinking about volunteering, most of us don't realize the skills we possess may be really important. Meet with the leadership of the nonprofit sharing what you do; for example, if you're an accountant, you could help with the books, if you're a lawyer, perhaps you can review/negotiate the next contract, marketing executive, you could design the next brochure. Standard pro bono services are valued at an average of $120 per hour according to a study by the Taproot Foundation. Volunteering — what a wonderful way to make a difference!

Making a Difference

John D. Rockefeller is credited with not only revolutionizing the oil industry but defining the structure for philanthropy in a modern world. He founded Standard Oil but did much more in philanthropy for his entire life. From his first paycheck, he tithed 10% to the church and later with Marshall Field co-founded the University of Chicago and several other educational institutions, medical causes, the arts and sciences. He spent more than 40 years doing great charitable work and making a difference that still influences our lives today!

Making a Difference

Thirty percent (30%) of American corporations have matching gift programs. They often "match" what an employee donates to charity; sometimes it's a 1:1 match, sometimes it's higher. Only 25% of eligible employees utilize these programs. It's estimated those who don't access it actually decrease donations by $1.5 billion! Check w/your company to see if it has a matching gift program. It could make a difference!

The Giving Pledge Campaign was

started by Bill and Melinda Gates as well as Warren Buffett during 2010. They have been meeting with other American billionaires asking them to donate half their wealth to charity during their lifetime or at their death. The results are the appeal has been well received with many taking the pledge! Thanks Bill, Melinda and Warren for leading by example and making a difference!

_____

_____

_____

_____

_____

_____

_____

_____

_____

Making a Difference

Jazzy Jordan ran 3159 miles across America! *California*
She started last Labor Day in CA and ran into NY Times
Square. The run was prompted by an employee of her
family's trucking company dying of cancer while medical
bills mounted. She ran to raise awareness about the
St. Christopher Truckers Development and Relief Fund
and the help it provides to truckers. She made a difference
with each step and mile!

Making a Difference

I learned about a 5th grader who raised $70,000 to help birds affected by the Gulf oil spill in 2010. Olivia Bouler cried when she learned from her grandparents about the birds being hurt by the oil. Then she took action drawing and painting pictures that the National Audubon Society sold for donations from $10 – 250. Folks learned about it, including those at AOL and it went viral. Now that's making a difference!

_____

_____

_____

_____

_____

_____

_____

_____

_____

Making a Difference

Do you remember McGruff the Crime Dog and his tips for safety? The National Council for Crime Prevention (www.ncpc.org) is still working to keep us aware and safe. After 30 years they're sharing tips on things such as traveling, identity protection and cyber-bullying. Their sole purpose remains in helping people, their families and communities remain safe from crime. NCPC continues to make a difference!

_____

_____

_____

_____

_____

_____

_____

_____

_____

Making a Difference

Linda Arye saw an opportunity where others saw only trash. One day she witnessed that discontinued fabric was being discarded into landfills. She saved that fabric and began making quilts for kids who had a life-threatening illness or were victims of abuse. That act and thought turned into the nonprofit Quilts for Kids (www.quiltsforkids.org). Check it out and learn how one (1) person makes a difference in the lives of children and those who help by simply making a quilt!

TIP OF THE DAY

Did you know most major sports teams have a charitable outreach program? Check out what your favorite team does to give back to the community. The Chicago Blackhawks, Stanley Cup Champions, work toward creating a better tomorrow for the youth of today. Since 1993, they have given away more than $7.5 million. Thanks to the Blackhawks for making a difference!

_____

_____

_____

_____

_____

_____

_____

_____

_____

_____

Making a Difference

The giving statistics for 2009 giving in the US were incredible! Individuals accounted for 88% of the $303 billion given away. Yes, giving by individuals, including through bequests and family foundations, account for the vast majority of donations. Most people are surprised by this statistic. But individuals, like you and me, REALLY do make a difference!!

_____

_____

_____

_____

_____

_____

_____

_____

_____

_____

_____

Making a Difference

How will you make a difference today?
My alma mater, Michigan State University, is tracking how alumni are changing the world. For example, did you know malaria kills 1 in 3 children annually in Sub-Saharan Africa? MSU graduates are working to prevent this and save the lives of young children. This might seem big but it started with an idea and a commitment. What can you do to make a difference?

Making a Difference

Texting while driving is dangerous! Oprah Winfrey is campaigning to end it by sharing stories of people who've been killed by a driver texting. More than 350,000 people have taken the pledge to stop texting or texting and talking while driving. Check out the stories and consider taking the pledge via Oprah's website. Consider making your car a "No Phone Zone". You will definitely be making a difference!

_____

_____

_____

_____

_____

_____

_____

_____

_____

_____

Making a Difference

One in three (1 in 3) people have been exposed to either Hepatitis B or C. Hepatitis is simply an inflammation of the liver and can be caused by a number of things. The World Hepatitis Alliance is a consortium of 280 groups working in this area. Learn more about this group and the 500 million people affected with hepatitis worldwide via the website; perhaps there's a way you can make a difference!

_____

_____

_____

_____

_____

_____

_____

_____

_____

_____

Making a Difference

In 2010 actor Joe Mantegna and White Sox Manager, Ozzie Guillen met to plan how they could raise awareness and funds to support the amazing work Easter Seals Metropolitan Chicago (www.eastersealschicago.org) is doing to help kids with autism! ESMC is building a state of the art, cutting edge, full service campus to help kids and their families. What an example....two very busy men are making time to make a difference!

_____

_____

_____

_____

_____

_____

_____

_____

Making a Difference

Actor Joey Travolta, John's brother, has a company called Inclusion Films. The company's goal is to provide developmentally disabled people with entry level knowledge of film production. I learned about this from Joe Mantegna who's oldest child has autism and is working in the film industry. Hats off to Joey Travolta for the good work he's doing to make a difference to a population often overlooked!

Making a Difference

Many think one person can't make a difference, but ask the students that receive scholarships because of Peter Travota. Peter started the Massachusetts Soldier Legacy Fund in 2004 after reading about a soldier who had died without meeting his unborn child. The MSLF helps children of fallen soldiers by providing scholarship dollars to help defray college costs. Now, that's making a difference!

Making a Difference

I found a great nonprofit website (www. Give2cents.org) that is interactive and helps the National Parks Conservation Association. Give2cents.org allows you to share stories of visits to national parks. Each word typed suggests a $.02 donation. It's easy, fun and a way to protect national parks so future generations can enjoy them! Check it out, share your stories, make a donation and make a difference!

Most college students *many* no longer fit the traditional student model. Most juggle school, work, family and the budget. Consider helping a non-traditional student. Contact a community college or four year institution to ask how you can help. Little things such as a book stipend, partial scholarship, daycare financial support do make a difference for all students, especially the nontraditional.

Making a Difference

April is National Poetry Month! It started in 1996 as a way to increase awareness and appreciation of poetry in the USA! When was the last time you read a poem? There are many nonprofits dedicated to keeping poetry alive and well. Check it out...poetry is an amazing literary form. Read a poem today and make a difference in your life!

_____

_____

_____

_____

_____

_____

_____

_____

_____

_____

_____

Making a Difference

Marshall Field was an entrepreneur and a philanthropist. In his day, he was a visionary building the Marshall Field and Company stores in the late 1800s. He believed in giving back to his community of Chicago. Through his involvement with the Museum of Natural History, it was named in honor of him becoming what we know today as the Field Museum. His philanthropic efforts continued when with John D. Rockefeller he cofounded the University of Chicago. They made a difference that continues to affect people today!

TIP OF THE DAY

Many of us plant vegetable gardens. Think about planting a "row" for your local food bank or pantry. By doing this simple act, you will be helping those in need and making a difference!

Making a Difference

When Albert Einstein was at Princeton University, it is reported the following statement hung on a sign in his office, "Not everything that counts can be counted, and not everything that can be counted counts." Focus on what matters and makes a difference. Do not worry about who gets the credit or who will notice...just do something today that makes a difference!

Making a Difference

Recently, I flew Southwest Airlines and learned something new about the company. They have the Medical Transportation Grant Program that provides free tickets to hospitals/medical transport organizations to distribute to patients and families traveling for medical care. In 2009, they increased the program by 20% now serving 30 hospitals and organizations nationally! They are definitely making a difference!

Making a Difference

Henry Ford once said, "Whether you think you can or can't, you're right." If you think you can't change the world you're right but imagine if you think you CAN change the world? What are you thinking about that could make a difference in your world?

Making a Difference

Did you know when there is a flood, such as the one that occurred in Nashville, Tennessee in 2010, people are in need of services to wash and dry clothes? The Tide Loads of Hope mobile laundry truck provides an opportunity for disaster victims to do their laundry. Now that's making a difference!

_____

_____

_____

_____

_____

_____

_____

_____

_____

_____

_____

Recently, I read about the Twilight Wish Foundation. This is a nonprofit granting wishes to low-income elderly people who are at least 68 years old or living in a nursing home. To date they have granted more than 1275 wishes through thirteen (13) chapters in twelve (12) states. Check out the website and consider finding a way to get involved. By helping to grant wishes you will be making a difference!

_____

_____

_____

_____

_____

_____

_____

_____

_____

_____

Making a Difference

The statistics are staggering. It is estimated that one in four women will experience some sort of domestic violence during their lifetime. Fifteen percent (15%) of US adults report having been abused. We must stop the cycle of abuse. To learn more or get help go to the National Domestic Violence Hotline website (www.ndvh.org). Become educated, learn how to identify the warning signs, empower yourself so you can begin making a difference!

Making a Difference

"Foster Kids are Our Kids" is a campaign in Illinois to raise awareness of the importance of the foster care system. It encourages us to think about becoming foster parents sharing why it is so important. Foster kids face many challenges often due to the fact their birth parents couldn't care for them. Learn more about foster care in your community. What could you do to make a difference?

Making a Difference

Many universities are offering social entrepreneurship courses. They find students want to start or work in businesses that do good. At the University of Michigan one project is for students to find a way to get fresh fruits and vegetables into convenience stores in Detroit. Now that's making a difference!

_____

_____

_____

_____

_____

_____

_____

_____

_____

_____

_____

TIP OF THE DAY

Did you know that kids receiving free or reduced lunches at school often are hungry because there might not be any food at home? Hunger doesn't just happen during the holiday season. It's a year round situation. Find your local food bank and consider making a donation or volunteering. You can make a difference in a child's life!

Making a Difference

Do you take care of your bones? For example, did you know people who break a hip and have surgery after the age of 70, have a 60% chance of living beyond the first year after the surgery? FEMR, a nonprofit, educates bout how we can begin taking care of our bones. Find out what you can do to prevent falls and take care of your bones. Begin making a difference in this area of your life!

_____

_____

_____

_____

_____

_____

_____

_____

_____

_____

Making a Difference

Haitian Wyclef Jean is working hard to keep the needs of Haiti and its people in the news. He fears we are all getting "Haiti Fatigue". I learned something new...did you know between 2000 – 3000 people have had amputations since the earthquake? There continues to be great need in Haiti. Consider making a donation to either Wyclef's nonprofit or another one that is working to make a difference!

Making a Difference

Recently, I had the privilege of learning about the Hopi Indian Nation. Did you know they set up an educational foundation with an initial donation of $10 million to benefit Hopi students attending college? Many students benefit from these funds and now are getting their degrees...with many returning home to help other Hopi Indians! Thanks to the leaders of the Hopi Nation for making a difference!

_____

_____

_____

_____

_____

_____

_____

_____

_____

_____

_____

_____

Did you know that Wal-Mart is the largest corporate cash contributor? In 2009, with in-kind services which include donations of food (64,000 tons) to food banks, they contributed more than $467 million to charity! Now that's making a difference!

Making a Difference

Nashville is still dealing with the aftermath from the rain and flooding in 2010! Do what you can to help....consider making a donation to the local food bank that is working to provide food to feed hungry people, first responders and volunteers! The website is www.secondharvestmidtn.org. You can still make a difference!

Making a Difference

Have you heard about 72 year old Daisy Brooks? She founded Daisy's Resource and Development Center in North Chicago (www.daisyrdc.com). This organization gives young pregnant women a place to live and attend school. In 2010 she was given the Presidential Citizens Medal, the nation's second highest civilian award because of this work. It inspires one to think, what can you do to make a difference in your community?

_____

_____

_____

_____

_____

_____

_____

_____

_____

_____

Making a Difference

The drugstore giant, Walgreens, loaned temporarily a prominent Times Square billboard to a charity! ~~It is~~ It is huge Jumbotron located on Broadway was used by the National Center for Learning Disabilities to run ads which were displayed on the 17,000 square foot digital video. The ads ran four (4) times an hour for four (4) days! What a way to make a difference! What can you do to help a nonprofit organization get its message out?

_____

_____

_____

_____

_____

_____

_____

_____

_____

_____

Making a Difference

Flooding has and continues to occur in our communities. When disaster strikes did you know local food banks supply the majority of food to the American Red Cross and other disaster responding organizations to feed the emergency workers and volunteers? Support your local food bank! You can find it by going to the Feeding America website (www.feedingamerica.org). You can make a difference!

Making a Difference

In 2009, the State of Michigan joined many other states and banned smoking in most public places. The new law will cover any workplace and any food service establishment including, but not limited to, restaurants, bars, shopping malls, bowling alleys, concert halls, arenas, museums, mechanic shops, health facilities, nursing homes, education facilities, and child care centers. Imagine the impact! What a way to make a difference in the lives of so many!

_____

_____

_____

_____

_____

_____

_____

_____

_____

_____

Making a Difference

In talking with the actress Patricia Arquette (star of the hit show Medium), recently, she told me about her work in Haiti. She is focused on insuring the 400 people in the village at Bois Neuf Field have clean water, water filtration systems, ecologically sound sanitation, hygiene and composting systems. The nonprofit is givelove.org; check it out and see how one person is making a difference for 400 people!

Making a Difference

Fisher Houses are a type of hotel where family members of soldiers can stay for little or no charge while their soldier is in the hospital. They are always full. After touring one of these houses, Denzel Washington asked what it would cost to build a new one. He then pulled out his checkbook and provided a donation to cover the costs! Talk about making a difference!

_____

_____

_____

_____

_____

_____

_____

_____

_____

Do you know the warning signs about teen dating abuse? The numbers are staggering such as one in five teens reporting having been hit, pushed or slapped by a partner while in a relationship; one in four report their partner tries to prevent them from spending time with friends and family. Learn more about the issue of teen dating abuse by going to www.loveisrespect.org and find ways to make a difference in a teen's life!

Making a Difference

Homelessness is still a big problem

in this country. I had the privilege of working with Bridge Communities, a model nonprofit helping homeless families (most headed by single moms) with transitional housing and other services such as mentoring, tutoring, etc. They work in DuPage County, Illinois but are fast becoming a national model. Check them out and see who is making a difference in your community by helping homeless families.

_____

_____

_____

_____

_____

_____

_____

_____

_____

Making a Difference

I saw an ad in a magazine recently featuring the actress Glenn Close and her family. The tagline read, "People told Glenn she was crazy to do this ad. She said, "Define crazy." Her response is because some of her family members have schizophrenia. As a matter of fact, one in six adults has a mental illness. Let's join Glenn and fight the stigma. Learn about mental illness and begin making a difference.

_____

_____

_____

_____

_____

_____

_____

_____

_____

_____

Making a Difference

I read recently about kids making a difference. Elementary age kids in Utah got the legislature to pass a resolution leading to signage at schools, airports and other high-idling zones telling drivers to turn off their engines after 15 seconds if they are not moving. The kids simply wanted to go outside and play but couldn't because of the smog... now they can! What a way to make a difference!

April is Autism Awareness Month. I saw a great ad in a magazine featuring singer Toni Braxton. It said, "Odds of having 3 multi-platinum albums = 1/1,650,000; Odds of having a child diagnosed with autism = 1/110!" Almost all of us know individuals affected by this condition. Learn more about the signs and affects of autism; with information you can make a difference!

Making a Difference

Oprah Winfrey is an American media personality most known for her award winning daily television show. However her philanthropic work is well known, too. She began Oprah's Angel Network, a charity that asks people to make a difference in the lives of the underprivileged with Oprah covering the administrative costs. From providing help during Hurricane Katrina to starting a school in South Africa for girls, Oprah Winfrey is making a difference!

Making a Difference

When Earth Day rolls around in the spring, do you have plans? What do you plan to do? I honor the day by speaking about the importance of being environmentally conscience. My staff takes the day to plan how we can be more environmentally aware in our office practices! That is how we are going to begin making a difference? How are you going to make a difference?

_____

_____

_____

_____

_____

_____

_____

_____

_____

_____

Making a Difference

In tough economic times, those who are in need often find comfort from their pets however, many are finding it a challenge to keep them. Consider making a financial or food donation to your local animal shelter to help those who are in need. Most communities have made arrangements for people to keep their pets. Investigate and find out how you help while making a difference!

_____

_____

_____

_____

_____

_____

_____

_____

_____

_____

Making a Difference

Be committed to the cleaning up the environment and keeping it clean. Make a plan. You are needed to make a difference!

_____

_____

_____

_____

_____

_____

_____

_____

_____

_____

_____

_____

_____

Making a Difference

Together we can save forests is the focus of Starbucks latest "do-good" campaign! Check out Starbucks website and view the 60 second film, "The Big Picture" (www.starbucks.com/thebigpicture#/film). It is an inspiring visual and details how by taking a single action we can make a huge difference!

TIP OF THE DAY

Annually in the spring there are days set aside as the Days of Remembrance — a time to honor the liberators of Nazi Europe and the victims of the Holocaust. Take time to learn more about what happened...read a book, attend a lecture, watch a program or visit a nonprofit website. By re-membering and learning more, you will help insure this type of atrocity does not happen again and make a difference!

Making a Difference

Never forget where you came from is a phrase we've all heard! A great example of this is New York Yankee Derek Jeter! Derek's foundation, "Turn 2 Foundation" promotes healthy lifestyles in kids and he does a lot for those kids in his hometown which is Kalamazoo, Michigan! Check out his foundation and the good work he's doing to make a difference!

Making a Difference

April 15th (or tax day as some of us call it) is a time of year for review. When looking for deductions have you included all you donated to charitable organizations? Charitable donations are still tax deductible. It is highly recommend to begin making a plan now for this year — determine how you will make a difference and also benefit by getting a tax break!

_____

_____

_____

_____

_____

_____

_____

_____

_____

_____

Making a Difference

I saw a sign on a bus that highlighted a company doing good. Levi Strauss Company has teamed up with Goodwill to get clothing to those in need! Check it out and see not only business doing good but also making a difference!

_____

_____

_____

_____

_____

_____

_____

_____

_____

_____

_____

TIP OF THE DAY

Public television is an amazing resource in our communities that most of us take for granted. Did you know that 80 million people every week watch public television (PBS)? It is important for it to stay around. Consider adding PBS (national or local) to your list of favorite causes. Make a donation today and make a difference!

Making a Difference

We all realize that education is important. Do you know the value added to that by attending a community college? Community colleges are often the best kept secrets in our communities and they have amazing resources! Check out the one in your community and see how they are making a difference!

TIP OF THE DAY

On Opening Day, most of us are aware or thinking of baseball! I recently learned about a great new museum honoring past players of baseball — the Negro Leagues Baseball Museum in Kansas City. It recognizes and preserves the rich history of African American Baseball. Check it out to see how many made a difference to the game we watch today! Play baseball!

April is Autism Awareness Month — did you know it is now estimated that 1 in 100 kids have some form of autism? Some think we are at an epidemic stage. Did you know Easter Seals is focused on helping kids and families live with autism? Check out the amazing work the Easter Seals Metropolitan Chicago is doing. They are truly making a difference!

_____

_____

_____

_____

_____

_____

_____

_____

_____

FLIP 126's 132

April 1st is considered April Fool's Day! Don't be fooled by fraudulent appeals for charity. Check out non-profits at the Better Business Bureau's Wise Giving Alliance (www.bbb.org/charity) or Charity Navigator (www.charity-navigator.org). See which nonprofits are really making a difference!

Wounded Warrior Project (www.

woundedwarriorproject.org) is a great nonprofit. Their mission is to raise awareness of the severely wounded service men and women. As they state, the greatest casualty is being forgotten. WWP puts together backpacks to deliver to the wounded when they return but are in the hospital. The backpacks contain some comforts of home including calling cards, music, gum, etc. Check out this amazing organization and read about a few people who seeing a need made a huge difference!

_____

_____

_____

_____

_____

_____

_____

_____

_____

Making a Difference

Did you hear about Marcia Merrick in Kansas City, Missouri? She was profiled in *People* magazine. At 4:30 am every morning she makes 400 sandwiches putting them in bags with chips, raisins and homemade cookies — and a note of encouragement. She distributes the food to the homeless everyday through her nonprofit www.reachingoutinc.org. Check it out to see how one person began making a difference!

Making a Difference

Have you thought about a career in the non-profit sector? More than 12 million work in this sector and when surveyed are happier and healthier than those working in the for profit and government sectors. Think about it! If you worked in the nonprofit sector, everyday you would be making a difference! What an amazing way to spend your work life — helping others!

_____

_____

_____

_____

_____

_____

_____

_____

_____

_____

Making a Difference

When Michael J. Fox was diagnosed with Parkinson's disease he was stunned. But he soon recovered and began aggressively fighting back. He started a nonprofit, the Michael J. Fox Foundation for Parkinson's Research. Its tagline is, "We don't just fund research. We fund results". Check it out at www.michaeljfox.org and help Michael make a difference by making a donation!

Making a Difference

People over 55 /*extra space* have a wealth of experience! Senior Corps is a nonprofit dedicated to connecting them with service organizations that can use their skills. Conceived during JFK's administration, more than 500,000 people serve as mentors, coaches and companions helping others in need. Check it out at www.seniorcorps.org; find out how seniors are making a difference!

Making a Difference

Did you know each night hundreds of thousands of families sleep on the floor or inappropriate places because they have no bed? The National Furniture Bank works to resolve that! They'll pick up your unwanted furniture for free and distribute it to families in need! They accept beds, dressers, tables, chairs, sofas, etc. Check out their website www.nationalfurniturebank.org; begin spring cleaning and make a difference, too!

Making a Difference

Have you ever wondered what to do with those bridesmaid and prom dresses filling your closet? Two suggestions: consider donating them to your local theater company — they are always looking for costumes. Alternatively go to www.donatemydress.org, a nonprofit giving dresses to disadvantaged teens looking for the perfect prom dress! Great ways to begin spring cleaning and to make a difference!

TIP OF THE DAY

The famous football coach, Vince Lombardi once said, "Individual commitment to a group effort — that is what makes a team work, a company work, a society work, a civilization work." What a profound statement. What can you do with a group today, this week or this month to make a difference?

_____

_____

_____

_____

_____

_____

_____

_____

_____

_____

_____

Making a Difference

Did you know that the month of May is National Bike to Work Month? People ride bikes for many reasons including for better health, saving fuel costs, contributing to a cleaner environment and staying off highways that are constantly backed up. Check out the website (www.bikeleague.org) to learn more. Consider adding bicycling to your summer schedule — you will be making a difference to yourself and your community!

Consider becoming an organ donor. Transplantation is really a modern day medical miracle!! Anyone can be a potential donor regardless of race, ethnicity or medical history. It is even said that all major religions support organ, eye and tissue donation. Consider becoming an organ donor today. You really will be making a life saving donation!

_____

_____

_____

_____

_____

_____

_____

_____

_____

Making a Difference

The singer/songwriter Tracy Chapman said, "I have seen and met angels wearing the disguise of ordinary people living ordinary lives." In other words, never judge a book by its cover or what someone can and will do for you by the way they look. Ordinary people make a difference every day!

Making a Difference

Did you know modern day slavery and sex trafficking still exists and is considered the second largest criminal industry with more than 12 million victims? The Polaris Project works for a world without slavery. It is one of the largest anti-trafficking organizations in the US and Japan. Check out the amazing work they are doing to make our world better and to make a difference!

_____

_____

_____

_____

_____

_____

_____

_____

_____

_____

Making a Difference

Ever wonder what to do with the old pairs of eyeglasses you have sitting around your house? One-Sight accepts all types of glasses in bins in many nationwide stores including Sears, Target, etc. They then provide the glasses along with eye exams to those who can't afford it throughout the world. Check them out at www.onesight.org and consider making a difference by donating your old used eyeglasses!

Making a Difference

Recently, I had the privilege of attending a spring training baseball game courtesy of the Chicago White Sox. Did you know they have an outstanding charity program? Annually, the Chicago White Sox manager (Ozzie), players and the overall organization give back to the community through a variety of programs including the White Sox Charities. Check out how they make a difference by going to their website (www.whitesox.com)!

Making a Difference

When the school year comes to an end, many parents wonder how to keep their kids busy and active during the summer. Consider having them take on a volunteer project this summer. Many nonprofits need volunteers. It could be a win-win situation for everyone. Talk to your child about what they would like to do and how they could make a difference!

Making a Difference

Ohio

It started with his father and uncle, now Wayne VanDoren and his family take up the tradition. Each Memorial Day weekend, they place flags on grave sites of veterans near their hometown of Clyde, OH placing over 1000 flags at one cemetery! It is their way of remembering and honoring those who have given their lives for the US! What can you do to remember and honor fallen heroes? Can you make a difference?

Making a Difference

TIP OF THE DAY

Oscar Hammerstein said, "There is a very real relationship, both quantitatively and qualitatively, between what you contribute and what you get out of this world." I agree...think about what you can do to make a difference. It just might change your life, too!

_____

_____

_____

_____

_____

_____

_____

_____

_____

_____

Memorial Day Weekend is always an opportunity to pause and remember those who gave their life in service to this country. There are many outstanding nonprofits working to honor and help current and past military people. Make a plan for this year's Memorial Day — do something to honor and remember those who gave their lives...attend a parade, visit a VA Hospital, meet with a veteran. You can make a difference!

Making a Difference

One of our American Founding Fathers, Benjamin Franklin, said, "When the well's dry, we know the worth of water." With government budgets tight, many social service and education programs are having their funding reduced. As a society, can we afford to lose these programs and their reach? Let's follow Benjamin Franklin's advice and know the worth of these things before they go away. Then, let's determine how we can make a difference.

Making a Difference

According to a Chinese proverb, if you want happiness for an hour, take a nap. If you want happiness for a day, go fishing. If you want happiness for a year, inherit a fortune. If you want happiness for a lifetime, help somebody. Consider having happiness for a lifetime by helping someone today! You will definitely be making a difference!

_____

_____

_____

_____

_____

_____

_____

_____

_____

_____

Making a Difference

Who was your favorite teacher in school? Do you remember the impact they had on your life? Mine was my second grade teacher, Mrs. Nancy Hall. Teachers make a difference everyday. Check out www.teacherscount. org whose mission is to raise the profile of teachers and provide resources. One of their taglines is, "Behind every famous person is a fabulous teacher"! Teachers do make a difference!

_____

_____

_____

_____

_____

_____

_____

_____

_____

Making a Difference

I saw a billboard recently for the Boys and Girls Clubs that had a photo of a very young Usher as well as Denzel Washington! Boys and Girls Clubs are embarking on a marketing campaign that can be found at www.begreatAmerica.org profiling celebrities and athletes and the fact they went to their local Boys and Girls Clubs when they were young! This nonprofit definitely makes a difference!

Making a Difference

If you could change the world, what would you do? Would you work to secure peace? Feed hungry people? Build better schools? Provide housing? In the United States, there are 1.5 million nonprofits doing work like this. Figure out what you want to do then find a nonprofit doing it — offer to help. You can volunteer, donate money or offer to be an advocate for the issue. You can make a difference!

TIP OF THE DAY

Have you visited the website of your local community foundation lately? Community foundations are a great resource often knowing the key issues that need to be resolved in your community. Check it out...they often provide ways for you to get involved and make a difference!

Making a Difference

The Olympics happen every two years alternating between the Winter and Summer Games. Watching and learning about the athletes always leaves many of us inspired. Studies are showing most of us want to "get in shape"! When thinking about a workout facility, consider your local YMCA (a nonprofit). Many have programs and facilities for exercising and they have joined the national "Let's Move" Campaign to end childhood obesity. Check out your local Y and begin making a difference on so many levels!

Making a Difference

Do you feel like there's nothing you can do to affect the environment? That in order to affect change, it would take too much time, cost too much money, etc. Here are some easy tips — turn off lights when leaving a room, shut off the water when brushing teeth and remove phone chargers from outlets when not being used. By doing things like these you can make a difference and help the environment!

Making a Difference

I recently checked into a Holiday Inn Express to find in my room a brochure detailing their partnership with Reading Is Fundamental (www.rif.org). Reading Is Fundamental is the nation's oldest and largest literacy nonprofit for children. It helps kids get a "smart start" to learn to read. Check it out and find ways to read to kids. You will be making a difference!

Making a Difference

During breakfast one morning, I noticed on the cover of the yogurt I was eating the words, "Give Hope With Every Cup". Dannon was committed to donating up to $1.5 million to fight breast cancer. Many companies align their products with a cause. It is a relatively easy way for you to make a difference — simply be aware and purchase products that donate a portion of the proceeds to charity. You can make a difference1

_____

_____

_____

_____

_____

_____

_____

_____

_____

_____

Making a Difference

Did you know that more than 3 million people in the United States live with epilepsy? The Epilepsy Foundation is a national nonprofit providing information and support to those living with this medical condition. Check out the website (www.epilipesyfoundation.org) to learn how you can make a difference to someone who has this condition.

_____

_____

_____

_____

_____

_____

_____

_____

_____

_____

Making a Difference

Recently a man shared with me the story of his daughter giving up three months of her life to go to Peru to help pregnant women. She was helping women learn about better health practices. He was amazed and awed by her willingness to give back at such a young age! What a shining example! But you don't have to go to Peru — what can you do in your neighborhood to make a difference?

_____

_____

_____

_____

_____

_____

_____

_____

_____

_____

Making a Difference

Most of us know pets bring comfort to many people. Did you know that many states are allowing dogs in the courtroom to help children who have to testify? It appears that the dogs have a calming affect on children who find themselves in this often stressful situation. What a way to make a difference!

_____

_____

_____

_____

_____

_____

_____

_____

_____

_____

_____

TIP OF THE DAY

I have just learned that a lot of women veterans have a difficult time when they return to the United States. It is estimated 6500 are homeless every night. Check out the nonprofit Iraq and Afghanistan Veterans of America (www.IAVA.org) as they do amazing things to help both female and male veterans returning from these wars. Perhaps you can find a way to help make a difference!

Making a Difference

We may not ever visit a food bank but we need to always remember there are hungry people all year round. Consider making a donation to your local food bank at a time of year other than the holidays. You can find one near you by going to the Feeding America website (www.feedingamerica.org). Make a difference in your community today!

_____

_____

_____

_____

_____

_____

_____

_____

_____

_____

_____

Making a Difference

Every 70 seconds, someone develops Alzheimer's with more than 5.3 million people having the disease in the United States. It is also the 7th leading cause of death. Check out more facts as well as the warning signs by visiting the Alzheimer's Association website (www.alz. org). There are ways you can get involved and make a difference to create a world without Alzheimer's.

_____

_____

_____

_____

_____

_____

_____

_____

_____

Making a Difference

Did you know that 200,000 children are homeless everyday? That 150,000 veterans are homeless at any given time and the fastest growing segment of our society that is homeless is families with children! We can do better! Check out the facts and how you can help by going to the National Coalition for Homelessness. By working together we can make a difference to end homelessness!

_____

_____

_____

_____

_____

_____

_____

_____

_____

_____

Making a Difference

Warren Buffet, the great Oracle of Omaha, once said, "Someone's sitting in the shade today because someone planted a tree a long time ago." This is a perfect description of philanthropy. Do something today that will affect someone years from now. Someone will benefit because of your actions. You will make a difference!

_____

_____

_____

_____

_____

_____

_____

_____

_____

_____

Many struggle to heat their homes during the fall and winter seasons. For those struggling with heating bills, please direct them to LIHEAP which is the federal "Low Income Heating Energy Assistance Program". This helps those who have a large percentage of their income going to heating. Contact your state LIHEAP agency to find out how to apply. Share this information; it could make a difference in someone's life!

Making a Difference

Have you ever watched the Olympics? Did you know there is a fundraising component associated with most of the US Olympic Teams? Yes, our athletes and the various teams raise money to compete. They do this through corporate sponsors and other fundraising means thus making a difference which allows us to enjoy the Summer and Winter Games!

_____

_____

_____

_____

_____

_____

_____

_____

_____

Making a Difference

Take care of your health — it is one of the most important things you can do! By leading a healthier lifestyle it is an example to young people in our lives as well as insuring as we grow older we remain healthy. Diabetes, heart disease, obesity, etc. are indicators of your health status. Think about what you can do today to begin living and leading a healthy lifestyle. Make a difference in your own life!

_____

_____

_____

_____

_____

_____

_____

_____

_____

_____

Making a Difference

Daniel Burnham, architect and Chicago city planner after the Great Fire in the late 1800s said, "Make no little plans. They have no magic to stir men's blood. Make big plans, aim high in hope and work." What big plans can you make today that will make a difference in someone's life?

_____

_____

_____

_____

_____

_____

_____

_____

_____

_____

_____

TIP OF THE DAY

Childhood obesity is at epidemic rates with 25 million, or 32% of kids and adolescents, being overweight. First Lady Michelle Obama is tackling this issue working with several departments to begin the www.letsmove.gov campaign. Check out the website. Think about healthy food choices and what you can do to make a difference in this battle with childhood obesity!

Making a Difference

John Johnson founded the *Ebony* and *Jet* publications which were the first to emphasize the achievements of African Americans. He later went on to build a cosmetic company, book publishing company, television production and purchase three radio stations. Through the Ebony Fashion Fair more than $47 million has been donated to charity. John Johnson and his many companies worked to make a difference!

TIP OF THE DAY

Did you hear about the hair stylist in New York who started giving the "unemployment haircuts"? Cristiano Cora who works in Manhattan normally charges $300 for a haircut (color and highlights are extra) but when the economy became challenging for most, he realized he could help. As he shared, "Everyone was stretching it...So I asked myself a very simple question: How can I help, what am I good at?" More than 100 jobless clients showed up the first day so he instituted a 'by-appointment' plan. Some clients weep upon seeing themselves with a decent haircut, some for the first time in years! Thanks, Cristiano, for making a difference!

Making a Difference

In 2010, the Serve America Act was passed by the Congress. The purpose of Fund is to increase the impact of social entrepreneurs and innovative nonprofit organizations through the scaling of programs and investing in promising new ideas. What new idea do you have that could be replicated to affect more people? How can your idea make a difference?

_____

_____

_____

_____

_____

_____

_____

_____

_____

_____

Making a Difference

Lisa Nigro, a former police officer, lives in Chicago and realized there were hungry people in her neighborhood so she started feeding the homeless out of a red wagon. Today, Inspiration Café and the Living Room Café offer a package of services to the homeless. In 2010, she was awarded the Presidential Citizens Medal, the nation's second highest civilian award because of this work. Where could you make a difference in your neighborhood?

_____

_____

_____

_____

_____

_____

_____

_____

_____

Making a Difference

Have you read the book *Three Cups of Tea* by Greg Mortenson? It chronicles his promise to a community that saved him. In 1993, Greg was attempting to summit the second highest mountain peak in the world and failed. Tired, he became lost from his group and stumbled into a village in Pakistan. Upon recovering, he made a promise to come back and build schools in an attempt to aid the peace process. Greg's story is an amazing account of how one person can make a difference! Think about a book that has made a difference to you.

_____

_____

_____

_____

_____

_____

_____

_____

_____

_____

Making a Difference

In 2010, the Chicago Foundation for Women
(www.cfw.org) celebrated its 25th anniversary. Founded
by four women with a vision in 1985, this group raises and
grants money to nonprofits focused on women's issues.
This example reminds us that sometimes a few people can
have an idea that makes a difference for many years!

TIP OF THE DAY

Little things really do matter. You can change someone's life by making a small donation, volunteering or sharing a story. You never know when your efforts will affect someone and make a difference!

Making a Difference

George Bernard Shaw said, "Life is no brief candle to me. It is a sort of splendid torch which I have got a hold of for the moment, and I want to make it burn as brightly as possible before handing it on to the next generation." He worked to make a difference and so can you. What could you do to keep the torch burning brighter while making a difference?

_____

_____

_____

_____

_____

_____

_____

_____

_____

_____

_____

Making a Difference

I love the Fourth of July!!! It is such a special day filled with celebration, steeped in history and an opportunity for communities to come together. When was the last time you celebrated Independence Day by attending a parade? Individuals in your community work hard to provide a celebration for the area. Your participation by attending and watching does make a difference! Go to the parade, the barbeque and the fireworks. Honor our Founding Fathers (and Mothers) and what they did to make a difference!

TIP OF THE DAY

I think bestselling author, Jim Stovall who wrote *The Ultimate Gift* summed up philanthropy when he said, "You need to be aware of what others are doing, applaud their efforts, acknowledge their successes, and encourage them in their pursuits. When we all help one another, everyone wins." Be aware and support others! You will be making a difference!

_____

_____

_____

_____

_____

_____

_____

_____

_____

_____

Making a Difference

Often times department stores will have an opportunity to shop and support a charitable cause. Macy's, Bloomingdales and Carson Pirie Scott have all had at least one day set aside annually where shoppers can purchase items and support a charitable cause or causes. Ask your favorite department store what they are doing to support nonprofits in the community and make a difference. Then consider shopping on that day and joining the effort to make a difference!

_____

_____

_____

_____

_____

_____

_____

_____

_____

_____

Making a Difference

Twenty-five (25) years ago, Willie Nelson, Neil Young and John Mellencamp formed an unlikely trio and founded Farm Aid, an effort to raise money and awareness of the plight of the family farmer. The overarching message is that America must support American family famers. Think about what you can do to support family farmers and make a difference!

_____

_____

_____

_____

_____

_____

_____

_____

_____

_____

_____

Making a Difference

Most of us have heard of Alcoholics Anonymous (AA) and the amazing work it does to help individuals struggling with alcoholism. Did you know it was founded by two men — Bill W. and Dr. Bob — in Akron, Ohio in 1935? The primary purpose of AA was to stay sober and help other alcoholics achieve sobriety. Since its founding, AA has helped millions of individuals struggling with the addiction on a daily basis. Imagine two men changing the lives of millions. Bill W. and Dr. Bob certainly made a difference. What can you do to make a difference to others?

Making a Difference

Pets are important to many people often providing comfort and joy. Many of us would like to add a dog or cat to our lives but wonder about the responsibility and costs. Consider volunteering to work with your local animal shelter to become familiar with the animals, their needs and local experts. When adopting a dog or cat, work with your local animal shelter to find the perfect animal. You will be making a difference!

Making a Difference

We hear about the rise of cyber-bullying almost every week. Cyber-bullying is when a child, pre-teen or teenager is tormented, harassed, threatened, humiliated or embarrassed by another child, pre-teen or teenager using the Internet or other technology tools including mobile phones. In other words, minor versus minor. Check out how to recognize and stop cyber-bullying by going to www.stopcyberbullying.org. See how you can make a difference!

_____

_____

_____

_____

_____

_____

_____

_____

_____

_____

Making a Difference

Many people wonder how they can make charitable gifts to nonprofit organizations if they have limited financial resources. Everyone can help...it just takes a little creativity. One idea is to consider purchasing extra products when doing your weekly or monthly shopping. Buying an extra roll of paper towels, an extra box of Kleenex or an extra can of coffee, will probably add little to your overall bill, but each of these items are needed and can be donated to your favorite nonprofit organization. Paper products, coffee, tea, creamer, reams of paper, etc. are items needed and by donating these you will be making a difference!

Making a Difference

David W. Packard had a vision. He recognized that the visual and audio recording arts (i.e., film, television and radio recordings) were one primary way in which our society would be viewed and studied in the future and that without preservation efforts these recordings could be lost forever. For example, over 65% of all television programs produced in America since the 1940s are not available in the public archives and may be lost forever. David Packard created and funded the Packard Campus for Audio and Visual Conservation which is dedicated to the preservation of film and audio recordings. Then he gave it to the Library of Congress! Thank you David for making a difference!

Making a Difference

Non-traditional recycling is an often overlooked way to give back to your community. Consider what you have in your home and how it can be re-used or recycled. Items such as clothes, electronics, furniture, etc. can be donated and will make a difference to those receiving them!

Making a Difference

Recycling is the process of turning a product's parts into another product and it saves the planet, your world and community! A number of cities and communities have made it easy to recycle and for that most of us are grateful. But even in communities where recycling has not been made "curbside" or "trash can" easy, consider this when we do not recycle at least our glass or aluminum we cost the earth in power usage, water and oil usage and landfill usage; for example, glass takes up to 4000 years to decompose in a landfill yet can be recycled indefinitely. Recycle and make a difference!

_____

_____

_____

_____

_____

_____

_____

_____

_____

Making a Difference

Mother Theresa said, "We can do no great things; only small things with great love." This is what philanthropy and giving back is all about. Doing small things that make a difference!

_____

_____

_____

_____

_____

_____

_____

_____

_____

_____

_____

_____

_____

Making a Difference

We all know Mark Twain was a prolific author. He is reported to have said, "Twenty years from now you will be more disappointed by the things you didn't do than by the ones you did do...Explore. Dream. Discover." This is an amazing and true statement. What do you think you can do to make a difference?

_____

_____

_____

_____

_____

_____

_____

_____

_____

_____

_____

Making a Difference

Born in December 1835, Phillips Brooks was a clergyman in Boston who during his life opposed slavery. He gave many sermons and offered many ideas about which to think including "Charity should begin at home, but should not stay there." How profound and true! What can you do to take your charity outside your home and make a difference?

_____

_____

_____

_____

_____

_____

_____

_____

_____

_____

Making a Difference

I was given a book by my friend Hallie Crawford titled *Little Museums: Over 1,000 Small (and Not-So-Small) American Showplaces.* It reminded me that there are hidden gems in our communities that need our financial and volunteer support. Go to your local museums, both big and small, to explore and learn more. Then consider becoming a supporter in order to insure they stay in your community and continue making a difference!

Making a Difference

In a 2003 issue of O Magazine, Kristin Hunter, a famous African American author, was quoted as saying, "First it is necessary to stand on your own two feet. But the minute a man finds himself in that position, the next thing he should do is reach out his arms." What a profound statement and so relevant. Are you standing on your own two feet? If yes, what can you do to reach out and make a difference?

_____

_____

_____

_____

_____

_____

_____

_____

_____

_____

Benjamin Franklin said, "Energy and persistence conquer all things." Use your energy and persistence to make a difference!

_____

_____

_____

_____

_____

_____

_____

_____

_____

_____

_____

_____

_____

The World Wildlife Fund (www.wwf.org)

and its campaign to save the tigers have a champion in the actor Leonardo DiCaprio. In the last 100 years, the wild tiger population has decreased by 97%! The goal is to double the number of wild tigers by 2022, the next Year of the Tiger in the Chinese calendar. Thanks, Leonardo, for making a difference!

_____

_____

_____

_____

_____

_____

_____

_____

_____

_____

_____

TIP OF THE DAY

Albert Einstein is credited with saying, "The world is not dangerous because of those who do harm but because of those who look at it without doing anything." What do you see that needs to be changed? How can you make a difference?

_____

_____

_____

_____

_____

_____

_____

_____

_____

_____

_____

Making a Difference

Frederick Law Olmsted is considered the father of American Landscape Architecture. He credited with creating the urban parks of Central Park as well as those in Boston, Chicago and Detroit to name a few. He made a difference through his work in the way many cities, college campuses and other communities are viewed today. Is there a way you can make a difference through the work you do?

_____

_____

_____

_____

_____

_____

_____

_____

_____

_____

Making a Difference

I love the book The Road Less Traveled by
Scott Peck and the message in the title. Reportedly Ralph
Waldo Emerson said, "Do not go where the path may lead;
go instead where there is no path and leave a trail." What
path can you take to make a difference in the lives of others? What nonprofit organization needs your help?

Making a Difference

An amazing national nonprofit has been started by my friend Margot Pritzker to encourage women to volunteer — Women On Call. The tagline is helping non-profits one hour at a time. Women On Call (www.womenoncall.org) is a unique online network that connects women to specific volunteer opportunities allowing them to share their professional skills and expertise with nonprofit organizations. Check it out and see if you can make a difference!

_____

_____

_____

_____

_____

_____

_____

_____

_____

_____

Making a Difference

The British Prime Minister Winston Churchill said, "The pessimist sees difficulty in every opportunity. The optimist sees the opportunity in every difficulty." What apparently insurmountable problem exists in your world? What is your attitude toward it? How can you make a difference and be the optimist that Winston Churchill references?

_____

_____

_____

_____

_____

_____

_____

_____

_____

_____

_____

TIP OF THE DAY

Philanthropy, charity, giving back, donating, etc. are all words that communicate helping someone else. Studies show that when you focus on helping someone else not only do you make a difference to them but a difference occurs in you. You will be amazed at how you feel by giving of yourself and your resources to someone else. Go make a difference today!

_____

_____

_____

_____

_____

_____

_____

_____

_____

_____

_____

Making a Difference

Listening. How often do you really do it? Everyone has a story. When did you last make the time to find out someone's story? You will be amazed at the difference it can make. Ask a senior citizen in a nursing ~~home~~ to tell you their story, ask the person who cleans your house or office their story, ask the new neighbor who moved in and really take the time to listen. Often times we are so busy telling our stories that we miss an opportunity to hear a great story. Do it and see the difference you will make!

Making a Difference

Most of us have heard of St. Jude's Hospital and the amazing work the actress Marlo Thomas continues to do on behalf of her family in supporting this outstanding organization. Did you know that hospitals who specialize in dealing with children's health issues often have active volunteer programs? The programs range from reading to the children to playing board games with them. Often there is a need for not only items such as board games, books, dolls, stuffed animals, etc. but also for volunteers. Check out your local hospital and see how you can make a difference.

TIP OF THE DAY

When was the last time you visited your local library? Libraries are an amazing place. Did you know that there are many ways to support your library? You can volunteer, donate the books you have already read and even read to children. Stop by your local library and see how you can make a difference!

Making a Difference

When many parents are getting their children ready for school, one key thing to remember is immunizations. August is National Immunization Month spotlighting the importance of keeping immunizations up to date for both kids and adults. When was the last time you checked your immunization records? It's a relatively easy way to make a difference and keep your community healthy!

_____

_____

_____

_____

_____

_____

_____

_____

_____

_____

_____

_____

_____

The singer/songwriter Bruce Springsteen is

a great philanthropist. Did you know in every city or town in which he performs a concert he makes a personal financial donation to the local food bank? Bruce Springsteen sets an excellent example of giving back! This is his tradition and way to make a difference...what can you do?

Making a Difference

High school class reunions are a wonderful time to reconnect and become acquainted with classmates. Why not consider adding a charitable component by raising money for a special need of your alma mater? Schools have many needs these days. Place a call or meet with the principal and ask what are the top three needs for the school. It could be something such as props for the drama department, new equipment for the physical education department or LCD projectors. Then work with your classmates to raise the funds or find the equipment. You definitely will be making a difference!

_____

_____

_____

_____

_____

_____

_____

_____

_____

Making a Difference

Have you heard about Ryka fitness shoes? Started by Sheri Poe in 1987, they shoes are designed by women for women! Ryka believes in giving back and has a long history of doing so to women's fitness that encourage women to go out and move to participate and be active. What a company...dedicated to doing good and to giving back. Ryka makes a difference!

_____

_____

_____

_____

_____

_____

_____

_____

_____

_____

Making a Difference

Did you see the movie, *The Blind Side*? It is well worth the rental. It is the story of a mom seeing a young man who had no place to live. Michael attended her son's school. This woman, Leigh Anne Touhy, brought Michael into her family and a transformation happened to the entire family. Everyone's life was changed and for the better! One simple act of kindness made a difference. Check it out and then think how could you make a difference in someone's life?

_____

_____

_____

_____

_____

_____

_____

_____

_____

_____

Making a Difference

I recently heard that philanthropy is a grown up word for sharing. I really like that definition. How can you be a philanthropist today and make a difference?

_____

_____

_____

_____

_____

_____

_____

_____

_____

_____

_____

_____

Making a Difference

Vince Gill is an amazing musician! He lives and works in Nashville having written and recorded numerous hit records. But what he is often more known for is his generous and philanthropic spirit. He is endearingly referred to as "Mr. Benefit" because of how often he says yes when asked to give back. Thanks, Vince, for making a difference and setting an example. What will you be asked to do today for someone else and can you say yes?

_____

_____

_____

_____

_____

_____

_____

_____

_____

Making a Difference

When was the last time you received a handwritten letter? If you are like most people, it has probably been a long time ago. Everyday I try to send one piece of personal handwritten correspondence to someone. I pay attention to what I read, those folks who are receiving awards or being recognized. Then I send them a note of congratulations. I try to make a difference in their life by sending a simple note. Who could you send a note today to make a difference? Could you commit to sending a piece of personal correspondence everyday?

_____

_____

_____

_____

_____

_____

_____

_____

_____

Making a Difference

The term dog days of summer refers to the days between late July and early September typically thought to be the hottest time of the year in the Northern Hemisphere. While we humans are trying to stay cool, be sure to look out for the animals. They, too, suffer in the heat. Volunteer at your local animal shelter during these hot days. You might find a new passion and will be making a difference!

Making a Difference

Katie Couric has done amazing things in her career interviewing thousands of individuals including the very famous and newly recognized individuals. She also almost singlehandedly raised the profile of colorectal cancer. Her husband, Jay Moneghan, died of it in 1999. Katie lived her life bravely as many other widows have done but also has worked tirelessly to insure that people are aware of this disease and what steps to take to prevent it. Katie Couric has definitely made a difference. What has happened in your family for which you could become an activist?

_____

_____

_____

_____

_____

_____

_____

_____

_____

Making a Difference

One of my favorite places in the world is the Country Music Hall of Fame and Museum located in Nashville, Tennessee. It is an amazing place with many artifacts including Elvis Presley's car, Johnny Cash's black suit and the Dixie Chicks costumes as well as lots of musical instruments. It is also an active museum conducting restoration of items and research into the country music genre. Did you know it is also a nonprofit? Most museums are a nonprofit. Consider supporting them by visiting, buying annual passes or making a donation. You can make a difference and insure your favorite museum is around for a long time.

Making a Difference

Are you looking for a family project? How about committing to a monthly charity project? Every month has many causes that can be discovered by doing a simply search on the Internet of the month + Charity Awareness. Create a family project and commit to doing something once a month to give back. You will be making a difference and teaching your children, too!

_____

_____

_____

_____

_____

_____

_____

_____

_____

_____

_____

Making a Difference

August is National Psoriasis Month. Many in my family suffer from this disease and it is really misunderstood. Psoriasis is a non-contagious disease of the immune system that appears on the skin and affects 125 million people worldwide and more than 7.5 million in the US! The singer Lee Ann Rimes went public with her battle with psoriasis and the toll it takes daily on her life. Learn more about this disease (www.psoriasis.org) and see how you can make a difference!

Making a Difference

Did you know the United States is often considered the most philanthropic country in the world? The USA was founded on the principles of philanthropy — of neighbor helping neighbor. There was no church or monarchy to build or provide for the schools, churches, orphanages, poor houses and libraries. In the beginning, it took a group of people in a community to decide something was needed and then to have the courage, strength and wisdom to make a difference! What do you see in your community that needs to be created, improved or changed? Gather a few people together and begin determining how you can make a difference.

_____

_____

_____

_____

_____

_____

_____

_____

_____

Making a Difference

Most of us have heard the stories of people collecting their loose change for a year in a jar or container and then when it is counted there is often a lot of money that has been saved. I challenge you to do that starting today. Collect your loose change for one year. Then, one year from today count it and decide to give half or all of it to your favorite nonprofit organization. What an easy way to make a difference!

_____

_____

_____

_____

_____

_____

_____

_____

_____

_____

Making a Difference

What do you do with your old prescription glasses? If you are like most people they stay tucked away in a drawer for years. Why not donate them? Sometimes the price of a pair of glasses in an African country can exceed three months pay. You can do something by donating your old eyeglasses. Drop them off at Goodwill Industries stores, Lenscrafter stores and Lions Clubs boxes. You will definitely be making a difference!

My stepfather developed diabetes as an adult. He had one of his legs amputated. He had been fitted for a prosthetic leg and over the years he had several "legs" made for him. When he died, my mom and I gathered his numerous prosthetic legs and donated them through the distributor to individuals in Developing and Third World Countries who don't have ready access to this medical device. While there was sadness in the visit with the distributor, there was great joy in knowing Don's prosthetic legs would help someone else. Even though he had died, he was still making a difference!

At times we read about unknown people who do random acts of kindness that get noticed by the news media. I often marvel at how a simple idea had a profound effect. Are you looking for something to do? A suggestion is to carry coins with you for the sole purpose of putting them in expired meters and helping people you don't know avoid getting a parking ticket. A simple way to make a difference!

Making a Difference

$\mathcal{L}ife\ can\ be$ full of challenges at times. I am always impressed with how people turn those challenges into opportunities to make a difference. What challenge are you facing today? Can you turn it into something that could make a difference for someone else?

_____

_____

_____

_____

_____

_____

_____

_____

_____

_____

_____

_____

_____

_____

Have you heard about KABOOM? KABOOM is a national nonprofit dedicated to kids' play. Their mission is to create play spaces through the participation and leadership in the community. KABOOM's overall goal is to have a safe place to play within walking distance of every child. Check out KABOOM at www.kaboom.org and see if you might want to become involved in creating great play spaces. You could make a difference for children in your neighborhood!

_____

_____

_____

_____

_____

_____

_____

_____

_____

_____

TIP OF THE DAY

The husband of a friend of mine passed away recently. When I saw her I told her how beautiful his life was described in his obituary. She told me that her husband always took the time to send a note to someone who was in trouble. Everyday he read the newspapers and learned about people, famous and not famous, those he knew and did not know, dealing with difficulties. After reading the stories, he would take the time to write a note telling them he was praying for them. This simple act made a huge difference to many, many people. Could you do something like this for others and make a difference in their lives?

_____

_____

_____

_____

_____

_____

_____

_____

_____

Making a Difference

I love the story of stone soup! It tells the tale of initially everyone hoarding what they had and not sharing even though everyone was hungry. The person who had carrots would not share the carrots; likewise for the person who had onions, potatoes, etc. One day, so the story goes, an old woman brought a huge pot to the middle of the town square and put water and stones into it. When asked what she was doing she said she was making stone soup. One by one everyone became curious and tried the soup. The person who had the carrots immediately recognized that the soup would be much better if it had carrots and went to get the carrots and add them, as did the persons with the onions, potatoes, etc. What a feast they ended up having! One woman had a vision and made a difference to an entire community. What can you do to make a difference?

_____

_____

_____

_____

_____

_____

Making a Difference

There is a saying that states if you give a person a fish they will eat for a day, but if you teach them to fish they will eat forever. Both types of actions are needed. What type of philanthropic action do you want to take? What type of change do you want to make? How can you make a difference today?

_____

_____

_____

_____

_____

_____

_____

_____

_____

_____

_____

_____

Making a Difference

Sometimes problems seem overwhelming. Hunger. Poverty. Child Abuse. Homelessness. Mental Illness. The list seems to go on and on. Often people are stuck because they do not know where to begin? Begin with one. Help one person today; help one person this week; help one person this month. Do what you can to make a difference in the area that is most important to you!

Making a Difference

If you were to die today, how would you want to be remembered? My guess is not by the type of house you lived in, the job you had, the car you drove or even the vacations you took. Like most people, you would want to be remembered for the difference you made. Keep that as your focus and find a way to make a difference in someone's life today!

_____

_____

_____

_____

_____

_____

_____

_____

_____

_____

Making a Difference

In large cities there are populations of homeless people often asking and sometimes begging for money. How do you treat these individuals? I find most people choose to ignore them or treat them disrespectfully by calling them names or yelling. I challenge you the next time a homeless person asks you for something to treat them respectfully. My response is often to look them in the eye and say, "No but thanks for asking me." It means I have recognized the person as a fellow human, heard their request and given them an answer (by the way, I choose to provide my support to nonprofit organizations that help homeless individuals). Even though I am not giving them money, I try to make a difference!

Making a Difference

As the President of the United States, Jimmy Carter was often criticized as was his administration. He served one term and did not get re-elected. Whatever your opinion of his Presidential service is, I think most of us would agree that his work in the nonprofit sector, especially with Habitat for Humanity has definitely made a difference and set an example for other leaders to follow.

Making a Difference

Do you know your neighbors? Have you provided help to them in the last year? Or asked them for help you need? If we begin being "neighborly" again we just might make a difference in our community!

Making a Difference

Winston Churchill, former Prime Minister of Great Britain, gave a speech consisting of six (6) words during World War II. It was "Never, never, never, never give up!" Do you have a dream for your community? Follow Winston Churchill's advice and don't give up. By being persistent, you just might make a difference!

_____

_____

_____

_____

_____

_____

_____

_____

_____

_____

_____

Making a Difference

By now, all of us have seen the yellow rubber band bracelets that have the words, "Live Strong" on them. Most of us know they are worn by people in support of the work the Lance Armstrong Foundation is doing. Their tag line is "We fight to improve the lives of people affected by cancer." An interesting fact shared on the website is that 28 million people are affected by cancer worldwide. Visit the website www.livestrong.org and learn more about how Lance and others are working to make a difference. What could you do today to make a difference to someone affected by cancer?

_____

_____

_____

_____

_____

_____

_____

_____

Making a Difference

Henry Ford, founder of Ford Motor Company, said, "One who fears failure limits his activities. Failure is only the opportunity to more intelligently begin again." People have shared their stories of disappointment and failure with me. Sometimes they state that they will never become involved with another charitable effort again. I think they should take Henry Ford's advice and begin again. You can make a difference but you have to keep trying!

Making a Difference

Do you remember the story about Osceola McCarty, the African American washerwoman, who at the age of 86, after spending her entire life hand washing, drying, ironing and folding clothing for $1.50 a bundle, walked into the Chancellor's office at the University of Southern Mississippi with a check for $150,000? She did this because she was committed to helping one child attend school. Osceola did not have the chance to finish her education, leaving school in the sixth (6th) grade to take care of a sick aunt. But she was committed to helping someone else. Most people probably thought she could never make a difference, but she did! In honor of Osceola, what can you do today to make a difference?

_____

_____

_____

_____

_____

_____

_____

Making a Difference

When summer is winding down and Labor Day is fast approaching consider making plans for your volunteer efforts this fall. In this tough economy many schools, as well as other nonprofits, need YOUR help! Take time to decide where you want to make a difference — your kid's school, the senior center down the street or by simply helping your neighbor prepare for the winter. Find a way to make a difference!

Making a Difference

John Muir is considered the "Father of the National Parks" in the US. He was an early promoter of the preservation of the wilderness he found and loved in the US. He lobbied Congress and in 1899 the National Park Bill was passed establishing both the Yosemite and Sequoia National Parks. John Muir had a dream and worked to make it come true! His efforts made a difference that affects all of us today. What are your dreams? What can you do to make a difference today?

_____

_____

_____

_____

_____

_____

_____

_____

_____

_____

Making a Difference

During the opening ceremonies of the 2010 Winter Olympics, the remake of "We Are the World" debuted. More than 80 artists came together to sing on this song. Consider purchasing this single knowing that the proceeds will continue to benefit the recovery efforts in Haiti. While it has been some time since the devastating earthquake, we should still remember and continue to make a difference!

Making a Difference

Did you know the first Labor Day was celebrated on September 5, 1882 in New York City? President Cleveland was committed to reconciliation with the labor movement after the Pullman Strike ended in a number of deaths. He made a difference! Today, we recognize Labor Day as the official end of summer with a day of rest and barbeques. Take today to consider things you can do to make a difference.

Making a Difference

Many of us have heard of the Montessori Schools but do you know how they were started? One woman, Dr. Maria Montessori, had an idea of how to educate "special needs" children. Upon finding great success in working with special needs children, she decided to also work with "normal" children. The end result of her work is the Montessori Schools. Educating for peace became a guiding principle for Dr. Montessori and because of her efforts she was able to make a difference in how children are educated. What can you do to make a difference in the life of a child?

_____

_____

_____

_____

_____

_____

_____

_____

_____

_____

While flipping through a magazine

I noticed the clothing line of Jones New York has a program called Jones New York in the Classroom (www.jyninth-eclassroom.org). During the back to school season, they have a produced a limited edition t-shirt that directs 100% of the profits to this charity which supports teachers and children's education! Check out how a clothing line is making a difference!

Making a Difference

Laughter is the best medicine. Most of us have heard this saying but Patch Adams lives it daily! Every year he gets other volunteers throughout the world to travel to other countries where they dress as clowns to bring humor to orphans, patients and others. Laughter makes the best medicine. Patch Adams and his friends make a difference! Laugh today and make a difference!

_____

_____

_____

_____

_____

_____

_____

_____

_____

_____

_____

I love the old riddle, "How do you eat an elephant? One bite at a time." It is good advice for how to tackle large and difficult problems in your community...one bite at a time in other words, one step at a time. You can make a difference...just take your time.

Making a Difference

Andrew Carnegie was a shrewd businessman finding great success and much wealth. In the latter part of his life he became a great philanthropist known for many things among which is his establishment of the Carnegie Libraries in the US, Great Britain and other English speaking counties. It was Andrew Carnegie's belief that libraries should be free to access. At the time, there was much debate about this with many thinking libraries should not be free. Andrew Carnegie led the way with words and deeds thus making a difference that benefits many today. Go to you local library and while browsing the stacks of books, say a silent thank you to Andrew Carnegie for making a difference!

Making a Difference

When I was a student at Michigan State University I was at a bus stop on Harrison Road. I needed to catch the bus in order to get to my job on time. As I was waiting, I noticed a blind man trying to cross the street. The traffic was heavy and it was likely he might get hit as he was not crossing in a crosswalk. I looked around and saw there was no one else to help so I asked him if he would like help crossing the street. He readily said yes then latched onto my arm and we began our trek across the street dodging speeding cars. While we had made it safely across the street, I realized I had left my book bag on the bench on which I had been sitting and as I turned to go back saw that the bus I needed to catch had stopped blocking my view of my book bag which was filled with all my belongings. With much trepidation, I started back across the street to see the bus pull away. As the bus bench came into view I saw another man sitting next to my book bag. When I got to the bus bench he said, "I saw what you were doing so I decided to sit here and watch your book bag." We had both missed our bus but we both were smiling because we knew we had made a difference!

Making a Difference

Howard Thurman said, "Don't ask what the world needs. Ask what makes you come alive, and go do it. Because what the world needs is people who have come alive." I love this statement because it is so true. Go and come alive...make a difference!

_____

_____

_____

_____

_____

_____

_____

_____

_____

_____

_____

Making a Difference

The first day of fall is an opportunity to "fall" proof your home! Did you know 40% of people who fall and break a bone after the age of seventy (70) die within a year of the fall? The Foundation for Education and Research of Musculoskeletal Research (FEMR) provides education and tips to "fall-proof" your home such as taping down rugs and keeping a flashlight beside the bed. FEMR is making a difference!

_____

_____

_____

_____

_____

_____

_____

_____

_____

_____

_____

Making a Difference

Have you ever heard the Starfish Story by Loren Eisley? The story goes that once there was a man who had retired. He rented a house on the beach and began thinking about his life deciding that no matter what he did, nothing ever changed. Even as he looked out at the ocean, he saw that hour after hour, day after day the waves came in and went out...never changing. Then one day he looked down the beach and saw a young man moving like a dancer. He smiled to himself at the thought of someone who would dance to the day, and so, he left the porch to check it out. As he got closer, he noticed that the young man as not dancing at all but he was reaching down to the shore, picking up small objects, and throwing them into the ocean. He came closer and called out "Hey there! May I ask what it is that you are doing?" The young man paused, looked up, and replied "Throwing starfish into the ocean." The older man than said, "Why are you throwing starfish into the ocean?" To this, the young man replied, "The sun is up and the tide is going out. If I don't throw them in, they'll die." Upon hearing this, the older man laughed cynically saying, "Young man, do you not realize that there are miles and miles of beach and there are starfish all along every mile? What difference do you think you could possibly make?" Without being deterred, the young man bent down, picked up yet another starfish, and threw it into the ocean. He then turned to the older man and said, "I made a difference to that one."

_____

_____

They say life is full of opportunities and chances. The charitable world is also full of opportunities and chances to make a difference. Take notice today of what opportunities exist and chances to make a difference. You might be surprised.

Making a Difference

Have you ever noticed other people in cars when you are driving? No one seems to be happy. Make a difference today by being a courteous driver? You could let someone in who is trying to merge, you could choose not to run a yellow or red light or you could simply choose not to honk your horn. Try to be a courteous driver for a day and you will make a difference!

_____

_____

_____

_____

_____

_____

_____

_____

_____

_____

Making a Difference

Moliere, the French playwright and actor, is credited with saying, "It is not only what we do, but also what we do not do, for which we are accountable." These are amazing words of wisdom from a long time ago philosopher that are still true today. You can make a difference both by what you do and what you don't do. Today, take time to notice what you do and do not do and how it affects others.

_____

_____

_____

_____

_____

_____

_____

_____

_____

_____

_____

Making a Difference

Family gatherings can be a stressful time. Many personalities and long histories can make things complicated. Why not try finding an activity everyone can do together that will make a difference...maybe cleaning up a park or river, working in a soup kitchen, visiting seniors in a nursing home, etc. Many, many ways to make a difference to not only others, but perhaps in your family, too!

TIP OF THE DAY

Today is the first day of the rest of your life. Many of us have heard this saying but it really is true. Each day is the first day and an opportunity to make a difference. What can you do today that will make a change in someone's life?

_____

_____

_____

_____

_____

_____

_____

_____

_____

_____

_____

_____

Making a Difference

Weddings are a great time of celebration. Why not add a charitable component? Some couples ask people attending their wedding to bring a nonperishable food item and collect them for a local food bank or food pantry. Some couples list their favorite charitable causes in the hopes that the wedding attendees will make a donation instead of brining a gift. What a unique and beautiful way to celebrate a new marriage and make a difference!

_____

_____

_____

_____

_____

_____

_____

_____

_____

_____

_____

Winston Churchill said, "We make a living by what we get, we make a life by what we give." Make a life and you will be making a difference!

_____

_____

_____

_____

_____

_____

_____

_____

_____

_____

_____

_____

_____

_____

Making a Difference

When was the last time you thanked a fireman for the work they do. These are individuals in our community who make a difference. Many small communities even have "volunteer" fire departments meaning people who say they will help in times of trouble and disaster. What a way to make a difference! Is there something in your community for which you could volunteer that would make a difference?

_____

_____

_____

_____

_____

_____

_____

_____

_____

_____

Making a Difference

Most of us have heard the phrase when life gives you lemons make lemonade. What has happened to you or your family that seems like lemons? What could you do that would change this situation into lemonade meaning what could you do with a tough situation that could make a difference?

_____

_____

_____

_____

_____

_____

_____

_____

_____

_____

Making a Difference

Many in our society are affected by mental illness. It is a term that describes a wide range of diseases yet many of us still don't know a lot about these illnesses. Take time to learn about mental illnesses and what you can do to make a difference. Sometimes just having knowledge about something will allow you to make a difference!

Making a Difference

Sixteen (16) years after the Plymouth Rock Pilgrims arrived in North America, we have our first documented act of philanthropy. Three men were sent back to England to raise money. One was hanged, one we don't know what happened to him and the third came back with 500 pounds and Harvard College (now Harvard University) was created. Because the pilgrims and early colonists did not want to continue sending their children back to England for an education they worked together to make education available in the new land. They certainly made a difference!

_____

_____

_____

_____

_____

_____

_____

_____

_____

Making a Difference

Many people who attend college are awarded educational scholarships to help them. Scholarships are created for a variety of reasons. They usually have criteria about to whom they should be awarded. Think about a scholarship you could create or perhaps one you received. Whether the donor or the recipient, scholarships make a difference in so many ways!

_____

_____

_____

_____

_____

_____

_____

_____

_____

_____

_____

_____

When was the last time you stopped by a child's lemonade stand? You see them often in the spring and summer. Stop by and buy a glass of lemonade. You will be making a difference to the child and you will be amazed at how good you feel!

_____

_____

_____

_____

_____

_____

_____

_____

_____

_____

_____

Making a Difference

We all have people in our lives that have had a positive effect on our lives. What most us do not do is tell them. Take today to think about someone who has made a difference in your life and then write them a letter telling them what they did that changed your life. Even if you can't locate them or they are deceased, write a letter to them that you know you will never mail but that will make a difference!

_____

_____

_____

_____

_____

_____

_____

_____

_____

_____

Making a Difference

Civic Clubs were a way that individuals in a community came together to make a difference. Do you belong to a civic club in your community? Check out the Rotary, Kiwanis, Elks and Moose Clubs. You might be amazed at the various things they do to make a difference.

Making a Difference

Dinner parties are a wonderful way to make a difference! It really doesn't matter what you serve for the meal, meaning if you make it simple or fancy. It is about bringing together people from different parts of your life who through meeting could make a difference! Think about hosting a dinner party at your house soon...bring together folks from different parts of your life and watch what happens!

Making a Difference

Most of us dream of taking exotic vacations to far away places but then wonder how we would ever get there let alone pay for it. Why not consider a voluntour vacation? A voluntour vacation is a vacation with an organized volunteer aspect. For example, you could travel to South Africa and during the week work to clean up an environmental ecosystem then on the weekends you could travel to the wine country to visit and vacation. You could travel to India and restore temples during the morning and sightsee in the afternoon. Check it out...there are a number of companies that organize these types of vacations...and they are tax deducible as a charitable donation. Think about it...you could make a difference while vacationing!

Making a Difference

I met an entrepreneur who is a donor to various charitable groups. He told me that when times get tough and his business is struggling, he takes out his checkbook and makes a donation to his favorite cause. He says it instantly makes him feel better and he knows he is making a difference. The side effect is that usually things start to shift in his business, too. What do you do when times get tough to make a difference? Consider doing something for someone else...you will be amazed at the difference you make for them and you!

_____

_____

_____

_____

_____

_____

_____

_____

_____

Making a Difference

Many of us have read the stories about a child or children being abused. If you are like most people, your heart aches and you wonder what you can do to help — consider becoming a CASA. CASA is an acronym for Court Appointed Special Advocates (www.casaforchildren.org). It began when a judge in Seattle, Washington realized that there was no one in the court system that was there for the child and only had the child's well being as their primary concern. Children and their interests can get lost and overlooked if no one is advocating for them! By becoming a CASA you will be making a difference!

_____

_____

_____

_____

_____

_____

_____

_____

Making a Difference

My Aunt Vivian was diagnosed with Multiple Sclerosis a few years ago. She has good and bad days but whenever I see her she is always smiling and has a kind word. That is what I notice about people with a life threatening or life altering illness. They often seem to value life more than those of us who have our health. Take time today to notice those around you in wheelchairs, using walkers and canes or struggling with an illness. Then notice their disposition. They make a difference by how they live their lives. What could we learn from them?

_____

_____

_____

_____

_____

_____

_____

_____

_____

Making a Difference

I love Starbucks! I love the experience of buying a coffee specially and specifically made to my tastes. But what I also appreciate about the Starbucks experience is the company's commitment to giving back. Check out the bottles of water they sell. The name of the water is Ethos and if you read the bottle, a portion of the purchase price is dedicated to helping children get clean water. It is a great idea to align their charitable strategy with their business strategy of selling beverages and an outstanding way to make a difference!

Making a Difference

Public

Do you listen to National Public Radio? If so, are you a member? Radio stations and programs depend on charitable donations for their operating and programming budgets. Consider becoming a member today. You wll be making a difference!

_____

_____

_____

_____

_____

_____

_____

_____

_____

_____

_____

_____

Making a Difference

Start today with your philanthropic and charitable activities. Most people, who are philanthropic and charitable, when asked state they wished they had started sooner! Start today and make a difference!

_____

_____

_____

_____

_____

_____

_____

_____

_____

_____

_____

Making a Difference

Women entrepreneurs say that philanthropy is more than just making a financial donation. It is a hug, a smile, shoveling someone's sidewalk, mowing a lawn, helping a neighbor bring in their groceries, etc. If you follow this advice, you can be a philanthropist today and every day! Look for ways that you can make a difference today!

_____

_____

_____

_____

_____

_____

_____

_____

_____

_____

_____

_____

Making a Difference

Most entrepreneurs interviewed say there is a difference between charity and philanthropy. Charity is more immediate and short term. Philanthropy is focused on the long term. Both are needed. What motivates you...charity or philanthropy. Think about it and then do something to make a difference today!

Making a Difference

What is your first philanthropic or charitable memory? When asked, most people respond by stating they remember seeing their mom or their family doing something around food during the holidays for those who are less fortunate. They recall making food baskets, buying food or working in a place, usually a house of worship, where a meal was served. What do you recall? How did it make a difference then and how does it affect you now?

_____

_____

_____

_____

_____

_____

_____

_____

_____

_____

TIP OF THE DAY

Theodore Roosevelt was the 26th President of the United States. He said, "In any moment of decision, the best thing you can do is the right thing, the next best thing is the wrong thing, and the worst thing you can do is nothing." Do something to make a difference!!

Making a Difference

When interviewed, entrepreneurs who are philanthropic state that a side effect of giving away money is that somehow they seem to make more money. I have heard a few say that the more they gave away, the more they made! It was an unanticipated outcome from their charitable activities. It seems their giving back makes a difference in a number of ways!

_____

_____

_____

_____

_____

_____

_____

_____

_____

_____

_____

I love asking people for money! I think there are only two answers they can give me: yes or no. When you are involved with a charity or nonprofit and asked to fund-raise do you dread it? Here is an easy tip: ask the person for permission to ask them for money. I know it sounds funny but it works. Try this: "Joe, the next time we meet I would like to tell you about a cause I care about and ask for your financial support. Would that be all right?" You will be amazed by the results you get and find you are easily making a difference!

Making a Difference

I went with my mom to her doctor's appointment for her heart check up. While she was in the exam room, I was in the waiting room. In the middle of the waiting room was a card table with a jigsaw puzzle on it and four chairs. I took a seat and began working the 1000 piece puzzle. Soon after the three other seats were filled, all of us silently worked to find pieces of the puzzle that fit. What amazed me was the way we worked. One of the puzzle players was randomly trying pieces in various parts of the puzzle; another was busy turning all the pieces up and separating them into color categories; a third was working only with straight edged border pieces and I was trying to find the box cover with the photo. It reminded me again of many ways we can approach problem solving. The charitable world at times seems like a puzzle that needs to be put together. I believe it is by all of us working together and utilizing all of our talents that we will continue to make a difference!

_____

_____

_____

_____

_____

Making a Difference

A few years ago, I went to my friend Jenny Porter's wedding in Mexico. Her parents, Nancy and Earl, had rented two buses for friends and family to travel from Tucson to the wedding destination. On a Thursday morning we boarded the buses and departed. Earlier in the week, Jenny asked me to be in charge of the bus with the family members and had written several suggested travel trip games. So we began the trip and decided to play one game called, "Two Truths and a Lie". The purpose of the game is for each person to stand up and make three statements of which two are true and one is a lie. Then the rest of the participants need to guess which one is the lie. The lesson I learned from this game is that everyone has a story! Often what seemed like the most outrageous statement is true (like when the groom's 60+ year old aunt said she had been a Dallas Cowboy Cheerleader — it was true!!!). Listen to people...ask them their stories...you will find out how they made a difference!

_____

_____

_____

_____

_____

Making a Difference

Did you know most food banks have at least four times the buying power you do? Think about it this way, when you go to the grocery store and buy $10 worth of food to donate it is a good thing. However, if you gave the food bank that $10 they could buy at least $40 worth of food because of their relationships with food manufacturers and vendors. A donation of $10 could be a great thing and make an even larger impact than purchased food. Two different ways to make a difference!

_____

_____

_____

_____

_____

_____

_____

_____

_____

Making a Difference

I heard a story about Charles Kuralt, the former CBS reporter and host of *CBS News Sunday Morning*. He shared that after interviewing one man they became friends. Every year after that interview the man invited Charles to his cabin to fish. Every year Charles said he declined citing one business obligation or another. This happened for about 15 years. Then one year there was no invitation. Charles wondered what had happened and was informed that man had died. Charles started thinking — what had been so important that he couldn't go fishing? He definitely did not remember the details of the work that put off the fishing trips. However, Charles did realize one thing... that if he had gone fishing he would have remembered that! Think about what you say yes to and what you decline. Then think about what really matters...what will make a difference in your life?

TIP OF THE DAY

The National Marrow Donor Program (NMDP) is focused on being a resource to help insure that all patients receive the bone marrow transplant need. I became a donor a few years ago when my friend Stephanie had a friend whose young son needed a bone marrow transplant. It was a simple and easy swab of my inside cheek. Check out Be The Match (www.marrow.org) to find out how you can become a donor. You will be making a difference!

Making a Difference

St. Vincent de Paul is reported to have said, "Charity is infinitely inventive." Most of us have heard about the Society of St. Vincent de Paul. We know of their thrift stores and that they do good work. But their mission is to embrace the network of charity. The members are young and old men and women who offer one-to-one service to those in need especially in area of poverty, suffering and loneliness. Twelve million (12) people are assisted by the Society members annually. Thank you for marking a difference!

Making a Difference

Most of us know of Anne Frank the young and brave girl who was killed during the Holocaust. After the war and her death, her diary was made into a book, one of the most widely read books in the world. Anne Frank said, "How wonderful it is that nobody need wait a single moment before starting to improve to the world." She made a difference and so can you! Make plans to read her book and learn how to make a difference!

Making a Difference

Mother Theresa said, "If you can't feed a hundred people, then feed just one." A wonderful mantra to live by...make a difference today by helping one person!

_____

_____

_____

_____

_____

_____

_____

_____

_____

_____

_____

_____

Making a Difference

My favorite quote of all time is by an anonymous person who said, "What would you attempt to do if you knew you could not fail?" Think about this as you try to determine what you will do to make a difference in the world.

_____

_____

_____

_____

_____

_____

_____

_____

_____

_____

_____

_____

_____

Making a Difference

I love the film Willy Wonka and the Chocolate Factory. A line uttered by Mr. Wonka speaks volumes, "So shines a good deed in a weary world." This line was adapted from William Shakespeare's *Merchant of Venice*. Whether written by Shakespeare or adapted by David Seltzer for the film, it is a good saying to remind us of the importance of doing good for it does make a difference!

_____

_____

_____

_____

_____

_____

_____

_____

_____

_____

Making a Difference

My friend Valerie Ingram is a mom to two elementary aged boys. With the budget shortfalls, she has seen cutbacks in supplies in the classroom. A few years ago, her youngest son's teacher approached her with an idea. He wanted to be green and instead of having paper towels for the students to dry their hands with he would prefer hand towels. He shared that if he could get 10 parents to each buy one hand towel, then he would have two for each day (one to use in the morning and one to use in the afternoon). Valerie listened to him and promptly told him that she would buy all the towels. As she recounted the story to me later in the week, she was still marveling at the look on the teacher's face. She said it was as if she had given him a large donation. Valerie made a difference that day and one that I bet the teacher will never forget nor will Valerie. What seemingly simple thing can you do today to make a difference?

Making a Difference

My father, Bob, loved boxing. I remember learning about Cassius Clay, now called Muhammad Ali, the great American boxer from him. Muhammad Ali said, "Service to others is the rent you pay for your room here on Earth." I find this a very profound statement about making a difference!

Making a Difference

The great broadcaster, Tom Brokaw, said, "It's easy to make a buck. It's a lot tougher to make a difference." Work today to do the tough thing...making a difference!

_____

_____

_____

_____

_____

_____

_____

_____

_____

_____

_____

Making a Difference

Robert F. Kennedy said, "Each time a man stands up for an ideal, or acts to improve the lot of others, or strikes out against injustice, he sends forth a tiny ripple of hope...and crossing each other from a million different centers of energy and daring those ripples to build a current that can sweep down the mightiest walls of oppression and resistance." This statement is so true. Think of a group of mothers who got angry about drunk driving and started MADD (Mothers Against Drunk Driving). They stood up for an ideal and made a difference!

Making a Difference

Many of my friends post this saying by Mahatma Ghandi on their Facebook page, "You must be the change you wish to see in the world." No truer statement was every spoken. Be the change, make the difference!

_____

_____

_____

_____

_____

_____

_____

_____

_____

_____

_____

_____

Making a Difference

My mom gives the best gifts. One day I received from her a little wooden square plaque that hangs on my bulletin board. It says, "She packed up her potential and all she had learned, grabbed a cute pair of shoes and headed out to change a few things." Follow this advice today and I bet you will make a difference in your world!

Making a Difference

I am fond of sayings. One day, I found this button and promptly bought it with the hopes of remembering its message. The statement written on the button was made by Pastor Martin Niemoller who was a victim of the Nazis. He said, "In Germany first they came for the communists and I didn't speak up because I wasn't a communist. Then they came for the Jews and I didn't speak up because I wasn't a Jew. Then they came for the trade unionists and I didn't speak up because I wasn't a trade unionist. Then they came for the Catholics and I didn't speak up because I was a Protestant. Then they came for me — and by that time no one was left to speak up." Find a way to speak up today for someone or something; you will be making a difference!

_____

_____

_____

_____

_____

_____

_____

_____

Making a Difference

Most of us have heard the phrase, "Pay it forward." It is the idea that when a good deed is done in order to repay it, you do a good deed for someone else. Just think if we all did this...what a difference it would make!

Making a Difference

I love this saying, "Instead of counting the days, make your days count." If only we would do this what a difference it could make in the world!

_____

_____

_____

_____

_____

_____

_____

_____

_____

_____

_____

_____

_____

_____

Making a Difference

I have learned a lot from many people including religious leaders. Fr. Turk Rooney was someone from whom I learned a lot. One thing he taught me I remember to this day. When discussing the Bible he asked me if I know what the word Bible meant. I gave him the usual answers and he smiled stating, "The word Bible is an acronym. It means Basic Information Before Leaving Earth." It made sense to me and I learned that if I follow a few of its teachings I could make a difference.

_____

_____

_____

_____

_____

_____

_____

_____

_____

Making a Difference

In the Bible, Matthew 17:20 it says, "...if you have faith as small as a mustard seed...Nothing will be impossible for you." In trying to change things it can seem overwhelming but if you have faith, you can make a difference!

Making a Difference

Helen Keller was an amazing woman who overcame unbelievable life circumstances. She is credited with saying, "Alone we can do so little; together we can do so much." What can you and your friends do today or this week to make a difference?

_____

_____

_____

_____

_____

_____

_____

_____

_____

_____

_____

Making a Difference

There are three ways, beside government funding, for nonprofit organizations to raise money. They are memberships, products and/or services and finally, philanthropic donations. The easiest money to raise is through philanthropic dollars. Ask your favorite nonprofit how they raise money then determine a way to make a difference by improving their fundraising efforts.

Making a Difference

When I lived in Hancock, Michigan I once hosted a dinner party. I decided for dessert I would serve a chocolate fondue with fruit. This decision was made partly due to a number of the guests being on a diet and also because it was first Friday in Lent and a number of the guests had given up chocolate. The problem was I didn't own a fondue pot nor did any of my friends have one I could borrow. So I called the local K-Mart store to ask if they sold fondue pots. The woman who was helping me via the phone said she would check. When she returned to the phone she told me there were no fondue pots for sale and that I would have to borrow hers. I responded saying, "If only it were that easy." She replied saying, "Why wouldn't you borrow it?" I said, "You don't know me. How could I expect you to loan me your fondue pot." She readily assured me she would and without ever meeting the woman, I borrowed and used her fondue pot. I had a lovely dinner party and told everyone the story about the woman working at K-Mart who made a difference in our lives. What stranger has made a difference in your life?

_____

_____

_____

_____

TIP OF THE DAY

Many hospitals and other organizations have thrift stores. Consider shopping at them and supporting your favorite cause. You will find unique items and treasures to purchase. And when you do this you will be supporting the nonprofit organization and making a difference!

Making a Difference

Martin Luther King, Jr. said, "Everybody can be great. Because anybody can serve. You don't have to have a college degree to serve. You don't have to make your subject and your verb agree to serve...You don't have to know the second theory of thermodynamics in physics to serve. You only need a heart full of grace. A soul generated by love." Find a way to serve today to make a difference!

_____

_____

_____

_____

_____

_____

_____

_____

_____

_____

_____

Children outgrow clothing very fast often times without wearing out the clothing. When your child or children have outgrown clothes consider giving them to someone whose children might benefit from them or to a thrift store. Either way you will be making a difference!

Making a Difference

What do Hank Aaron, Bob Dole, Osceola McCarty, Colin Powell, Gary Sinise and Elizabeth Taylor

have in common? They are all recipients of the Presidential Citizens Medal which is the second highest civilian award in the United States. It was established in 1969 and its criteria states it can be given to any US citizen, "...who has performed exemplary deeds or services for his or her country or fellow citizen." Thanks Hank, Bob, Osceola, Colin, Gary and Elizabeth for making a difference!

Making a Difference

Helen Keller was amazing. She is quoted saying "No pessimist ever discovered the secrets of the stars, or sailed to an uncharted land, or opened a new heaven to the human spirit." Be an optimist today...see the glass as half full instead of half empty. If you do, I can guarantee you will start to see places you can make a difference!

Making a Difference

People often ask me when the first fundraising appeal was; in other words how did sending a written request to someone asking for money begin? The oldest recorded fundraising appeal was written by St. Paul around 55 A.D. It was an appeal to church members in Greece to help the impoverished members in Jerusalem. The appeal describes the benefits of giving. While we have no record of the results, I am sure we can believe money was raised and the effort made a difference!

_____

_____

_____

_____

_____

_____

_____

_____

_____

_____

Making a Difference

Did you know that people who regularly attend a house of worship are twice as likely. to give to charitable causes then those who do not attend? It is often through belonging to a house of worship that we learn how to give and how to make a difference.

_____

_____

_____

_____

_____

_____

_____

_____

_____

_____

_____

_____

Making a Difference

The great poet Maya Angelou is credited with saying, "I've learned that you shouldn't go through life with a catcher's mitt on both hands. You need to be able to throw something back." This is a very true statement. Give something back and make a difference!

_____

_____

_____

_____

_____

_____

_____

_____

_____

_____

_____

_____

Making a Difference

Did you know the working poor are the most generous Americans giving a larger percentage of their income to charity and charitable endeavors? We often think that only wealthy people give money to charity but that is not true. All individuals, regardless of income level, can and do make a difference!

_____

_____

_____

_____

_____

_____

_____

_____

_____

_____

_____

_____

Making a Difference

The second most generous economic group in the United States are the wealthiest Americans. While they are second to the working poor, they do better than the middle class donors. There is room for improvement for those of us in the middle class. Let's do better by giving more to charity. By doing this we will really make a difference!

Making a Difference

Did you know research shows that donors to charity are more likely than those who do not give to donate blood, help the homeless, give up their seats on a bus or train, give directions to strangers and even return excess change to clerks when purchasing products? Donors truly do make a difference in all aspects of their lives.

317

Studies show that people who give to charity are happier than those who do not. Give to charity...be happy while making a difference!

Making a Difference

Research show that donors are healthier than non-donors. They respond to surveys saying their health is excellent or very good! Become a donor...you will see yourself as healthier and be making a difference in a number of ways!

Research and studies show that people really do make more money for every dollar donated. It is estimated that the return on investment for each chartable dollar given is $3.75. Make a donation today...you will make a difference in so many ways!

_____

_____

_____

_____

_____

_____

_____

_____

_____

_____

_____

_____

Making a Difference

Abraham Lincoln is remembered as the 16th President of the United States. He provided a vision for tackling issues that is worth remembering. He said, "The probability that we may fall in the struggle ought not to deter us from the support of a cause we believe to be just; it shall not deter me." Let's follow in President Lincoln's footsteps. Don't worry about falling, work to make a difference!

Have you heard of VolunteerMatch? Founded in 1998, VolunteerMatch is a tool for individuals who want to volunteer and for nonprofits looking for volunteers. The mission of VolunteerMatch is to strengthen communities by making it easier for good people and good causes to connect. Check it out at www.volunteermatch.org and see how you might be able to make a difference!

Making a Difference

Mary Anne Radmacher is a writer and artist who said, "Courage doesn't always roar. Sometimes courage is the little voice at the end of the day that says I'll try again tomorrow." Don't give up too easily on your dream of making a difference...sometimes it just takes courage!

Making a Difference

Lung cancer is the #1 cancer killer of women. It is more deadly than the six (6) next largest cancer killers combined. You can help. Check out the Lung Cancer Foundation of America at www.LCFAmerica.org and see how you can make a difference! Let's work together to stop deaths by lung cancer among women!

_____

_____

_____

_____

_____

_____

_____

_____

_____

_____

_____

Making a Difference

Kenneth Cole is well known for his brand and is becoming well known for his philanthropy. In 1987, he started his involvement with amFAR which is the Foundation for AIDS Research. In an interview in the *Town & Country* magazine he stated, "There was an extraordinary stigma then with regard to HIV issues. The presumption was that if you were active in AIDS causes, you were a drug user, gay and/or Haitian, none of whom were exactly socially well-integrated into society. I wasn't any of those, but I stayed involved, eventually becoming chairman in 2005." Thank you Kenneth Cole for setting an example and making a difference!

We have all heard of the Nobel prizes that are awarded each fall. Do you know the history of how they began? It is reported that in 1888, Alfred Nobel's brother died while visiting Cannes and a French newspaper erroneously published Alfred's obituary. What surprised Alfred was that the article condemned him for his invention of dynamite. It said, "Dr. Alfred Nobel, who became rich by finding ways to kill more people faster than ever before, died yesterday." Saddened by what he read, Alfred wondered how he would be remembered. It is believed that this article prompted his decision to leave a positive legacy after his death. On November 27, 1895, Alfred Nobel signed his last will and testament setting aside the bulk of his estate (estimated to be valued at $250 million in 1896) to establish the Nobel prizes. Thanks Alfred Nobel for making such a huge difference in the lives of so many!

Making a Difference

Oprah Winfrey said, "Lots of people want to ride with you in the limo, but what you want is someone who will take the bus with you when the limo breaks down." I love this statement by Oprah and it describes perfectly how people want to jump on the bandwagon when there is success. That is good but when you are trying to make a difference you want someone who will be there when you are having success and when you are facing challenges, in other words when you are riding the bus. Find supporters who will be there to help you make a difference!

Lucille Ball was an outstanding comedian,

actress and human being. She said, "I don't know anything about luck. I've never banked on it, and I'm afraid of people who do. Luck to me is something else: hard work — and realizing what is an opportunity and what isn't." Sometimes we wish for luck like when we play the lottery in the hopes that if we won we could do things to make a difference. According to Lucille Ball you don't need luck, but hard work. Work hard to make a difference!

Making a Difference

"Injustice anywhere is a threat to justice everywhere", according to Martin Luther King, Jr. What injustices do you see in your world, in your community, in your life? Starting today work to make a difference where you see injustices occurring.

_____

_____

_____

_____

_____

_____

_____

_____

_____

_____

_____

_____

Making a Difference

Dale Carnegie said, "You can make more friends in two months by becoming genuinely interested in other people than you can in two years by trying to get other people interested in you." People have stories. Ask questions. You might be surprised at what you learn and find a way to work together to make a difference in the world!

Making a Difference

The famed artist Georgia O'Keefe stated, "When I was born and how I have lived is unimportant. It is what I have done with where I have been that should be of interest." In other words, Georgia is asking to be viewed and perhaps even judged by what she has done and how she made a difference!

Making a Difference

According to Mother Theresa, "Do not wait for leaders; do it alone person to person." What can you do to make a difference to one person today?

_____

_____

_____

_____

_____

_____

_____

_____

_____

_____

_____

_____

_____

Making a Difference

We have all heard the saying if at first you don't succeed, try, try again. Carol Burnett, the famed comedienne said, "I have always grown from my problems and challenges, from the things that don't work out, that's when I've really learned." The message I take from this is for people to continue to try to make a difference in their world even if they fail the first or second time.

_____

_____

_____

_____

_____

_____

_____

_____

_____

_____

_____

Making a Difference

Julia Child loved to cook! She discovered this passion while living in France and took the steps to perfect it. She had a huge impact on cooking. Julia said, "Find something you're passionate about and keep tremendously interested in it." She definitely made a difference!

Making a Difference

Most of us recall, Mr. Rogers and his show, Mister Rogers Neighborhood which was geared to children. However, there were many great life lessons for all of us. He once said, "The thing I remember best about successful people I've met all through the years is their obvious delight in what they're doing...and it seems to have very little to do with worldly success. They just love what they're doing, and they live it in front of others." Discover what you are passionate about, do it and have fun making a difference!

Making a Difference

Helen Keller said, "While they were saying among themselves it cannot be done, it was done." How often do you hear people saying what cannot be done? Do something today to make a difference living Helen Keller's faith!

_____

_____

_____

_____

_____

_____

_____

_____

_____

_____

_____

_____

TIP OF THE DAY

Stephen R. Covey is credited with saying, "Things which matter most must never be at the mercy of things which matter least." What matters most in your life? Focus your energies on it show you can make a difference!

_____

_____

_____

_____

_____

_____

_____

_____

_____

_____

_____

_____

_____

Making a Difference

Sometimes I am amazed at how some people think certain jobs are below them. I have always thought that no matter what the task was at hand as long as I did it well, I would always have a job. I came across a quote from Harry S. Truman the 33rd President of the United States. He said, "I found that the men and women who got to the top were those who did the jobs they had in hand, with everything they had of energy and enthusiasm and hard work." Now that is the way to make a difference — to do every job with energy, enthusiasm and hard work!

_____

_____

_____

_____

_____

_____

_____

_____

Making a Difference

Lee Iacocca is credited with saving the Chrysler Corporation in the 1980s. In 1982, he began work to save the Statue of Liberty leading the fundraising efforts to restore this American symbol as well as Ellis Island. He said, "So, what do we do? Anything. Something. So long as we just don't sit there. If we screw it up, start over. Try something else. If we wait until we've satisfied all the uncertainties, it may be too late." Lee Iacocca made a difference in business and philanthropy!

Making a Difference

The National Underground Railroad Freedom Center opened in Cincinnati, Ohio in August 2004. The building is just a short distance from the banks of the Ohio River which was the natural border between free and slave states until the Civil War ended in 1865. The Museum details the history and the roads traveled by many slaves escaping slavery. But it also has exhibits highlighting modern day problems such as human trafficking. Check out this new and wonderful museum; learn how people helped people escape a terrible life to find freedom...learn how they risked their lives to make a difference!

Making a Difference

Mark Twain said many memorable things but in reading this one I laughed out loud and realized I vehemently disagreed. He said, "Few things are harder to put up with than the annoyance of a good example." Good examples lead to people realizing they can make a difference. So, sorry Mark Twain...I disagree and love stories about good examples.

_____

_____

_____

_____

_____

_____

_____

_____

_____

_____

_____

TIP OF THE DAY

Here is a suggestion to remind you that many in the United States and the world do not have enough to eat. Set an empty plate at your dinner table once a week. Leave it there to remind you and your family of the struggle other people face in trying to secure enough food. Have discussions about what you and your family can do to make a difference.

_____

_____

_____

_____

_____

_____

_____

_____

_____

_____

Making a Difference

It was Senator John F. Kennedy's vision and challenge to a group of students at the University of Michigan that began what we now know as the Peace Corps. He asked the students to serve their country in promoting peace by living and working in developing countries. That challenge has developed over the years with more then 200,000 volunteers working in 139 countries and there still is more work to do. Check out the Peace Corps (www.peacecorps.gov) and see how you could make a difference!

Making a Difference

Holidays can be a time of great stress and chaos. Personalities and histories come alive when many people come together. Why not make a plan to change the focus this year from family dynamics and dysfunctions to differences that can be made. Host family discussions either in person or online to make suggestions of what could be done as a family to make a difference!

_____

_____

_____

_____

_____

_____

_____

_____

_____

_____

Making a Difference

Have you heard of Jennifer Nettles? She is half of the successful country music duo known as Sugarland which has had much success in the music industry. Jennifer credits music with helping her cope with a difficult moment in her childhood. She believes music was a safe place to let out her emotions and if it could do that for her, it could help others. With all the budget cuts to the arts and music, Jennifer has teamed up with Eddie Owen, founder and manager of Eddie's Attic in Georgia and launched the nonprofit Attic Community Playground. The purpose is to develop and underwrite arts curricula for schools. Thanks Jennifer and Eddie for making a difference!

Making a Difference

Breast cancer for women is a frightening diagnosis and disease. However, thanks to the Susan G. Komen for the Cure nonprofit great strides in research are being made. This foundation, like many others, came about because of a promise between sisters. In 1977 when Suzy was diagnosed at age 33 with breast cancer her sister Nancy was there as a rock of support. After three years and numerous surgeries, chemotherapy and radiation, Nancy made a promise to her sister that she would do something to help others battling this disease. The result is the Susan G. Komen for the Cure, a nonprofit organization that is the global breast cancer movement. Check it out at ww5.komen.org and see how you can make a difference.

_____

_____

_____

_____

_____

_____

_____

_____

Making a Difference

Paws is a nonprofit organization started in 1967 by a group of people dedicated to helping animals. They have done amazing work and their mission is to be a champion for animals. Their vision is to create a world where the intrinsic value of animals is recognized and behaviors toward animals is changed. Check it out at www.paws.org and learn how you can make a difference through your knowledge and treatment of animals.

_____

_____

_____

_____

_____

_____

_____

_____

_____

_____

Making a Difference

I love this statement by Martin Luther King, Jr., "Even if I knew the world would end tomorrow, I would plant a tree today." What would you do today even if you knew the world would end tomorrow? How would you make a difference?

_____

_____

_____

_____

_____

_____

_____

_____

_____

_____

_____

_____

Making a Difference

What was your favorite book as a child?
Do you remember it? Share it with others...give it as a gift
to the children in your life. Tell them why it made a difference to you.

Making a Difference

I love birthdays and I love celebrating birthdays! I find them a great opportunity to do an assessment of the past year and to make plans for the next year. This year on your birthday make a plan to make a difference.

I encourage you to share it with others; perhaps they will follow your lead and work to create a plan to make a difference on their birthdays, too!

_____

_____

_____

_____

_____

_____

_____

_____

_____

_____

_____

Making a Difference

Robert Frost, the great American poet, wrote, "Two roads diverged in a wood, and I — I took the one less traveled by, and that has made all the difference." Take the road less traveled and make a difference!

_____

_____

_____

_____

_____

_____

_____

_____

_____

_____

_____

_____

_____

Making a Difference

I read Cokie Roberts book *Founding Mothers*, several years ago and was amazed how it not only detailed what the women did to secure independence from England but how often it referenced fundraising activities by the early female colonists. One reference specifically stated that at the outset of the Revolutionary War, the Women of America (a group formed to support the effort) determined that they wanted to contribute as much as possible to securing the independence of the colonies. The plan was a fundraising effort on behalf of the soldiers. Early Colonial American women made a difference in their day. What can we do today to follow their lead and make a difference!

Making a Difference

Sometimes people tell me that trying to make a difference at times seems impossible. The problem is too big, there are not enough resources, etc. I like what the singer Beverly Sills once said, "There are no shortcuts to any place worth going." Tackle the problem and continue working to make a difference!

Making a Difference

Have you heard the daffodil story? First published in 1995 it is a true story about a field of daffodils in someone's yard in California. Many, many people have visited and are awe-struck asking who did this and how did it happen. It is reported that as you approach the patio to the house of the woman who owns the yard there has *is* a sign that says "Answers to the Questions I Know You Are Asking". It further reads the first answer was *is* a simple one. "50,000 bulbs"; the second answer was *is*, "One at a time, by one woman. Two hands, two feet, and one brain."; the third answer was *is*, "Began in 1958." It is amazing that one woman made a difference through her commitment, dedication and attitude. What can you do to make a difference?

_____

_____

_____

_____

_____

_____

_____

Making a Difference

I love going to the Farmers' Market. It is such a simple way to insure good food is on my table and that I am helping the farmers. Try to visit your local farmers' market...you will be making a difference!

Making a Difference

The 16th President of the United States, Abraham Lincoln, said, "I do the very best I know how — the very best I can, and I mean to keep doing so until the end." Living by this statement would insure that you make a difference... can you do it?

_____

_____

_____

_____

_____

_____

_____

_____

_____

_____

_____

Making a Difference

It is said every day each of us produces four (4) pounds of trash/waste. To do my part to help the environment I use cloth napkins instead of paper napkins in an effort to reduce the waste I produce. Historically cloth napkins were developed when people ate with their fingers. That napkin ring was designed later to hold an individual napkin so that each person knew which cloth napkin was theirs for the next meal as they only were given one for several meals. Today, cloth napkins are easily accessible. I encourage you to consider if you could incorporate using cloth napkins into your life, reducing your trash/waste and definitely making a difference!

_____

_____

_____

_____

_____

_____

_____

_____

Making a Difference

Former First Lady Rosalynn Carter said,

"A leader takes people where they want to go. A great leader takes people where they don't necessarily want to go but ought to be." What a profound statement. Think about the causes that today are accepted but at their beginning were rejected....AIDs, civil rights, recycling, etc. They had great leaders who showed others how make a difference!

_____

_____

_____

_____

_____

_____

_____

_____

_____

_____

Making a Difference

We all see the red kettles of the Salvation Army during the Christmas holiday season. Did you know the Salvation Army is an international movement and the evangelical part of the universal Christian Church? They work to meet human needs without discrimination and in that they are definitely making a difference!

Making a Difference

American journalist Charles Kuralt said, "The greatest thing you can do in life is to tell a young boy or girl that they're 'the very best' at something — baseball, reading, art. That gives them the wonderful feeling that they can do anything — which they can!" Words do matter...use them to make a difference!

Making a Difference

Did you know socks are important to the overall health of people, especially homeless people? Most homeless people do not have shoes that properly fit making socks even more important. However, socks are often not donated to shelters and if they are not in the quantities needed. Socks are relatively inexpensive. Consider purchasing new socks or collecting used, clean socks and donating them to the local shelter in your community. This is an easy and inexpensive way to make a difference!

I saw a public service announcement by created by CBS Cares with Mark Harmon discussing the bipolar disorder. In the ad he stated that it usually takes years to diagnose this illness which can be misdiagnosed as depression or other medical conditions. Learn more about the symptoms of bipolar disorder and how having knowledge can empower you to make a difference!

Making a Difference

I read in the newspaper about a six year old boy named Carson who loved to help his mom in the kitchen with the cooking. After a while they came up with the idea of a cookbook for kids written by kids. They also believed it would be a good way to teach children about hunger in the world. With this goal in mind, Carson went to school and asked his classmates for recipes of their favorite foods; the word spread and in the end the Carson and his mom compiled 800 recipes into the book, "Kids Feeding Kids". The proceeds from the book, $20,000+ were donated to the Northern Illinois Food Bank to be used in their youth nutrition program. Now that's taking a simple idea and making a difference! What idea do you have that could make a difference?

_____

_____

_____

_____

_____

_____

_____

Making a Difference

Leave No Veteran Behind is a new nonprofit started by two veterans (www.leavenoveteranbehind.org). The goal is to help other veterans battle their educational debt. As the website says, "...many service members who receive higher education during, before, or after their service have to take out costly loans to pay for their education. While there are military educational programs that help relieve this educational debt, not all veterans are covered under these programs. Leave No Veteran Behind addresses this issue by taking private donations and applying them directly to veterans' student loan accounts. In return we require that all veterans helped through our program give back 100 hours of community service." What a vision and an important way to make a difference!

Making a Difference

I love tossing stones in a pond or lake.
I love seeing the concentric circles of ripples travel outward from the initial toss. It always reminds me of how one act can have long lasting effects or ripples beyond what we see. While we often don't know what happens when we do something, be assured, every attempt to make a difference has a long lasting effect...just like tossing a stone in a pond or lake!

_____

_____

_____

_____

_____

_____

_____

_____

_____

_____

_____

_____

Proof

Made in the USA
Charleston, SC
07 November 2010